The Violin

The Violin

Its physical and acoustic principles

PAOLO PETERLONGO

Member of the National Academy of St Cecilia, Rome

Translated by Bill Hopkins

Foreword by
NORBERT BRAININ

Paul Elek London

First published in Italy in 1973 by Edizioni SIEI, Milan (in Italian and French)
© SIEI ing. Peterlongo–Milano 1973

First published in Great Britain 1979 by PAUL ELEK LIMITED
54–58 Caledonian Road, London NI 9RN

This revised edition © Dr.-Ing. Paolo Peterlongo 1979

This translation © Paul Elek Limited 1979

Colour photography by A. Papafava dei Carraresi (Plates I–IV, VII–XIV) and Zonda (Plates V, VI)

ISBN 0 236 40142 4

Typeset in Monotype Bembo by Ronset Limited, Darwen, Lancashire

Text printed in Great Britain by
Unwin Brothers Limited, The Gresham Press, Old Woking, Surrey
Colour plates and accompanying text, pages 129–60 printed by
Athesiadruck, Bozen, Italy

To the memory of my father

Contents

Figures

Acknowledgement

In the preparation of the present edition of this book, reference has been made to the German edition, *Die Streichinstrumente, und die physikalischen Grundprinzipien ihres Funktionierens*, published by Verlag Das Musikinstrument, Frankfurt-am-Main, 1976 (© Verlag Das Musikinstrument 1976) as well as to the first edition, *Strumenti ad arco: Principi fisici del loro funzionamento/Les Instruments à archet: Principes physiques de leur fonctionnement*, published in Italian and French by Edizioni SIEI, Milan, 1973.

Foreword by Norbert Brainin

In his book *The Violin* Dr Paolo Peterlongo explains the principles according to which string instruments function.

He does not explain the principles of violin construction, particularly not those by the great exponents of the art of violin-making of the classic Italian period. Neither does he explain the actual application of these principles of the construction of string instruments in practice. To attempt this would be like trying to explain the workings of the universe.

He mentions the so-called 'mysteries' and 'secrets' of the classic makers, which he easily explains as great artistic talent, taste, experience, immense skill and sheer hard work.

He makes us realize that violin-making is essentially an art because, in spite of the very exact known principles involved, the many unknown interacting factors make it impossible (according to Dr Albert Einstein) to arrive at an acceptable mathematical formula.

Dr Peterlongo further points out that everything connected with the violin, be it the bridge, the sound-post, the end button, even the weight of the scroll, etc, has a bearing on the tonal and aesthetic qualities of the instrument; that violin-making presupposes a profound knowledge of the practical application of the principles involved, a faculty which has evidently been lost over the years. It is in this field that the Italians and among them the Cremonese were and are the supreme masters.

That Dr Paolo Peterlongo should have been able to convey all this in a work on the scientific principles of the functioning of string instruments will be to his everlasting credit. It bears witness to his great love and limitless admiration for the works of the great masters of the classic period of Italian violin-making, but above all it bears witness to his humility.

February 1979

Author's Preface

There exists an art in which painting, inventiveness, and physical and acoustical science are ingeniously combined with constructional craft; an art which saw its highest flowering several centuries ago in Italy, where it attained a position of absolute and undisputed supremacy. This art is that of violin-making.

It is the aim of this brief study to explain the physical principles and functioning of bowed stringed instruments, and at the same time to pay tribute to all master violin-makers.

The greatest Italian violin-makers produced their masterpieces between the middle of the seventeenth and the middle of the eighteenth centuries. Here we will name just two of them: Antonio Stradivari and Giuseppe Guarneri del Gesù. These names are known wherever music is played and loved; they have a meaning for everyone, and are an inspiration to the artist.

In the course of time sceptics, imitators and innovators have appeared in violin-making, yet none has been able to overshadow the name of Stradivari and the other great masters of Cremona. Their creative genius, by nature both circumspect and methodical, enabled them to produce unrivalled masterpieces, and their supremacy remains undisputed to this day.

When it is considered that the violin and the other instruments of the violin family, and those of the great Cremonese makers above all, are in effect perfect 'machines' which have not been essentially improved for three hundred years, we can only marvel the more at the achievements of these artists in technique.

Paolo Peterlongo

I

Introduction

To perfect that wonder of travel—the locomotive—has perhaps not required the expenditure of more mental strength and application than to perfect that wonder of music—the violin.

W. E. GLADSTONE

Between the middle of the seventeenth century and that of the eighteenth the art of violin-making attained its finest flowering in Italy. It was during this period that the greatest Italian makers created their masterpieces.

The Amatis, the Guarneris, the Stradivaris, the Bergonzis and the Guadagninis, to name but a few, were all active at this time. But there were many others besides. All of them achieved such skill in violin-making that their creations can stand for all time as models of perfection in the art, and must inevitably be taken into account by anyone today wishing to examine stringed instruments from a scientific and technical viewpoint. Their instruments provide evidence that in their time nothing was left to whim or to considerations of mere aesthetic appearance. By examining a stringed instrument of the period, both in its entirety and in its individual parts, it is today easy to ascertain just how much intuitive skill, knowledge and experience—doubtless the fruits of a long tradition—these craftsmen possessed. Even details that may appear unimportant at a cursory glance will stand up to the most rigorous scientific investigation.

Anyone who is concerned with violins, violas and cellos should find it interesting and useful to be aware of how a stringed instrument functions mechanically and acoustically. A number of topics this book will deal with may already seem familiar or obvious to the reader. The explanations of physical and acoustical matters are in no way intended to provide guidelines for actually making a stringed instrument. Neither is it the purpose to expatiate upon how stringed instruments are constructed: that is the prerogative of the makers, who can speak on the subject with authority.[1] The sole purpose here is to explain how a stringed instrument functions and to demonstrate how the constituent parts affect the acoustic quality and sonority of the instrument as a whole.

15

The violin and the other stringed instruments are none of them the work of a single man, an 'inventor'. The construction of stringed instruments was brought to perfection by violin-makers over a period of time as they increased their understanding of the principles of acoustics and gradually became conversant with the rational use of materials.

Acoustical theory was already being taught in Italian universities at the time of Galileo (1564–1642). Galileo, the son of a composer, was himself a writer on music much occupied with the study of musical theory. It is very probable that Gasparo da Salò, Diffenbrugger and the Amatis knew something of acoustics and put this knowledge to such effect that their work contains what some would still today call the 'secrets of violin-making'. In fact, such 'secrets' were nothing more than the expression these makers gave, consciously or unconsciously, to their artistic talent and taste, added to what they had learnt from experience and tradition. All these are essential factors that have nothing in common with the empiricism prevalent today in certain factories and with certain violin-makers. There is no place for mass production methods or for standardized blueprints in the making of a good violin; for stringed instruments are made of living, natural materials. The characteristics of the wood from which they are made will differ from one piece to another, particularly when it is not taken from the same tree trunk. But the great makers of the seventeenth and eighteenth centuries were often fortunate enough to be able to use wood from the same pine and maple trees throughout an instrument.

The 'secrets' of the master violin-makers were the same as the principles which guided Michelangelo and Leonardo da Vinci to perfection. But in their case no-one imagines 'secrets' or ' mysterious forces' to have been at work.

In the present writer's estimation, each of these violin-makers possessed above all a methodical approach, balanced judgment and the priceless asset of being able to work in peace. The aura of mystery in which violin-makers of the past have frequently been shrouded is based on nothing more than widespread ignorance. They would have been amazed to read all the things that have been written about 'secrets' which for them never existed.[2]

Around the middle of the last century, F. J. Fétis, Director of the Brussels Conservatory, wrote a treatise on Stradivari and stringed instruments for the Parisian violin-maker Vuillaume.[3] He began with these words:

Italy, that land so fertile in things great and beautiful; Italy, in her civilization foremost among all the nations of Europe; Italy, finally, to whom has been granted every kind of glory in poetry, in philosophy, in the sciences and in the arts; Italy, I say, has been the cradle of those artists who have carried to its highest perfection the art of building bowed musical instruments. As early as the middle of the fifteenth century this art was already being successfully cultivated. Whence had it come? What causes lay behind its development up to the point where, in the hands of Antonio Stradivarius and of Giuseppe Guarnerius, called Del Gesù, it reached its utmost limits? Why has it declined with their successors?

There are periods in history which have been especially fertile for one or another of the arts and have seen great artists being born almost simultaneously; one need only think of the Renaissance in Tuscany, with Michelangelo, Leonardo and Raphael all contemporaries in sixteenth-century Florence.

In the eighteenth century, music began to be enjoyed beyond small confined circles, and better-designed and more sonorous stringed instruments began to be needed for performance. The great violinists and composers of the time, such as Vitali, Corelli, Vivaldi, Telemann, Handel and Bach, who were contemporaries of Stradivari and Guarneri, were much in need of instruments for their numerous pupils. Chamber music ensembles were already being formed in this period, to be followed by the first orchestras; the golden age of opera had its beginnings early in the century. There was a growing demand for strength and quality of instrumental sound.

According to Bacchetta,[4] Monteverdi (1567–1643), who was the son of a violin-maker and became a pupil of the violinist Ingegneri, was already in his day able to order increasing numbers of instruments for various orchestras from his home town of Cremona. He was in a position to do this because he had the support of the Gonzaga family, as well as later becoming *maestro di cappella* at St Mark's, Venice and commanding considerable influence at the courts of Florence, Ferrara and Rome.

Cremona at this time was exceptionally fertile ground for the development of the art of violin-making. It was the workplace of a large number of craftsmen in wood who had become specialists in marquetry.[5] It is quite conceivable that some of these craftsmen turned increasingly to violin-making.

From a glance at a map of the town centre (Fig. 1) it is strikingly apparent how close together were the various workshops of the most celebrated violin-makers. They all lived between the Contrada Cultellar and the Piazza San Domenico during the period from 1690 to 1750. The prospective buyer could choose whether to order his instrument from Amati, Stradivari, Guarneri del Gesù,

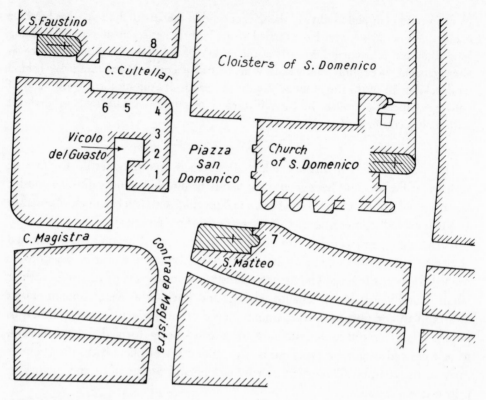

Violin-makers' workshops

1 - A. Stradivari, 2 - C. Bergonzi   3 - D.G. Guarneri,   4 - A.G. Amati
5 - L. Storioni, 6 - C.B. Ceruti, 7 - N. Amati, 8 - F. Ruggeri.

Fig. 1   The centre of Cremona (*c.* 1730), showing violin-makers' workshops

Bergonzi or Ruggeri. The best makers had so much work that even an emissary from a king or a prince would have to await his turn for weeks or even months before his goods were delivered.

From Cremona the art of violin-making spread throughout Italy, notably to Venetia, Campania, Piedmont and Lombardy. In that enviable age it was possible to work in peace and seclusion. There was time to ponder and to experiment in the workshop. Violin-makers were able to learn from experience, steadily improving their craft from one instrument to the next, and whenever possible making use of wood from the same tree trunk. The knowledge and experience they gradually amassed became an unwritten tradition of workmanship. Thus a kind of 'school' came into being, and its most brilliantly gifted exponents rapidly soared to fame.

2

The Violin-maker's Art

The common ancestor of modern stringed instruments was the viola. The smaller version of it which later came into being was called the violin. This instrument possibly represents the only man-made product to have undergone neither improvement nor modification of its form in the course of three hundred years.

Every other product of mankind has been continually evolved and perfected over the centuries; in contrast, the violin, the viola, the cello and the double bass achieved their definitive form shortly after the year 1700.

Since that time the instruments of the great Italian masters have remained without equal. They are of such perfection as to compel wonder in anyone fortunate enough to be able to make a close inspection of them. These master-pieces even fascinate many music-lovers not specifically involved in violin-making, but who wish to learn more about it once they have had occasion to admire these instruments.

In this and the following chapters, the members of the violin family will be discussed primarily from the point of view of physical acoustics. And although specific reference will be made to the violin only, the information given may be taken to apply to the viola, cello and double bass too—with due allowance for differences. So as not to trespass upon the realms of practical instruction, any points not essential to an understanding of the physical, mechanical and acoustical aspects of the subject will be studiously avoided.

The history of civilization has given ample proof that art and science, intuition and experience, are indissolubly linked. The Italian master violin-makers practised an all-embracing art comprising elements of architecture, of sculpture, and even of painting. At the same time it required of them an adequate knowledge of acoustics and certain branches of mechanics and physics, as well as some knowledge of chemistry in relation to the treatment and preparation of wood and varnish.

The violin, the viola, the violoncello and the double bass are complex constructions. The basic function of stringed instruments is to transform mechanical into acoustic energy. They operate in accordance with the principles of sound. These principles have long been known, and the most important of them are simply perceived, but the same cannot be said of their practical application.

Even Einstein—a sound musician who took a keen interest in acoustical problems associated with the violin—admitted that he knew no way in which mathematical formulae could be used to express the principles involved in designing and constructing violins. He declared that in this connection 'the present state of our knowledge does not enable us to explain anything'.

Everything that goes to make up a stringed instrument—not just the strings, the bridge, the belly and the other structural parts, but even the weight of the scroll and the tailpiece—has some effect on the fullness and quality of the instrument's sonority. Such details as, for instance, the position, the angle and the shape of the sound-holes, which are often thought of as unimportant, are on the contrary vital factors in determining the sound an instrument will make. The effect of the bow's action is to set in vibration the entire violin, in all its parts. The old masters understood this well, and that is why, when examining their instruments, a modern violin-maker will do well to look for the reasons behind the forms and physical characteristics of the whole and of the parts, rather than simply copying them blindly.

A stringed instrument, moreover, is just as fragile and temperamental as the human body, and, like it, is subject to disorders. And in exactly the same way that a good doctor will prescribe appropriate treatment only once he has made a thorough examination, so a good violin-maker should set about remedying the deficiencies of an old instrument that is in need of repair only after examining it scrupulously. Particularly in the case of instruments dating from the seventeenth and eighteenth centuries, it is inadvisable to undertake any radical alterations. Too many instruments have already been permanently ruined simply because an inexperienced maker has wanted to impose his own ideas on a stringed instrument constructed according to principles he has not begun to discover or understand.

We might start with Baglioni's definition:[1] 'The ideal stringed instrument is that in which the resonance chamber forms a system by which each note in each register will be amplified in equal measure.'

The complex shape of the body of a stringed instrument, with its curves and corners forming zones of larger or smaller compartments of air, represents a happy compromise in achieving this end. This shape creates a combination of resonators which will amplify with equal effectiveness both sequences of single notes and different notes sounding simultaneously. The smaller zones of resonance amplify the high notes whilst those of greater volume amplify the low notes. The best soundboard will be one that will induce vibrations of equal strength in the different resonators at various points of the instrument's body.

There is a real art in finding the ideal proportions that should obtain between the thickness and curvature of the belly and the back, and in the overall shape of the body of a stringed instrument, which will determine the volumes of air in different parts of the resonance chamber. To do this successfully, the violin-maker needs to possess judgement, a methodical attitude and reflective powers in the highest degree, so that he may give due weight to every requirement. It was precisely in these respects that the great makers of Cremona were true masters.

3

Nomenclature of Parts

It may here be of help to the non-specialist to name the constituent parts of the violin and other instruments of the violin family. The instrument shown in Fig. 2 is the violin, but apart from differences in dimensions, the structure and nomenclature remain identical for all four members of the family.

The violin has a wooden *body* which can be thought of as a box having a very special shape.

The upper side of the instrument, its *belly*, is made of pine. Its broader parts are sometimes known as the *upper* and *lower bouts*, with the *centre bout*, or *waist*, in between. The edges are reinforced with *purfling*. Two openings carved in the belly are known as the *sound-holes*.

The rear side of the instrument, analogous in shape to the belly, is called the *back* and is usually made of maple. The back and the belly are of different thicknesses, and are carved in arch form with the aid of special templates.

Fig. 2 shows the positions of the *bridge*, the *bass bar*, which is a longitudinal reinforcing bar of pinewood glued to the underside of the belly, and the *sound-post*, which is a small pinewood rod wedged between the back and the belly.

The *ribs* form the side wall of the resonance chamber. These are thin strips of wood, usually matching that of the back, reinforced where they join the front and back by the *linings*. The ribs are joined to an *upper* and *lower block* and four *corner blocks*. The upper block also serves as a means of securing the *neck* to the body. A hole is bored in the lower block for the insertion of the *end button*. The *tailpiece* is attached to the end button by means of the *tailgut* which passes over the *saddle*.

At the upper end of the *neck* is the *pegbox* into which the *pegs* are inserted, and the decorative *scroll*. The *fingerboard* is glued to the neck, and at its narrow end the strings pass over the *top-nut*.

The Violin

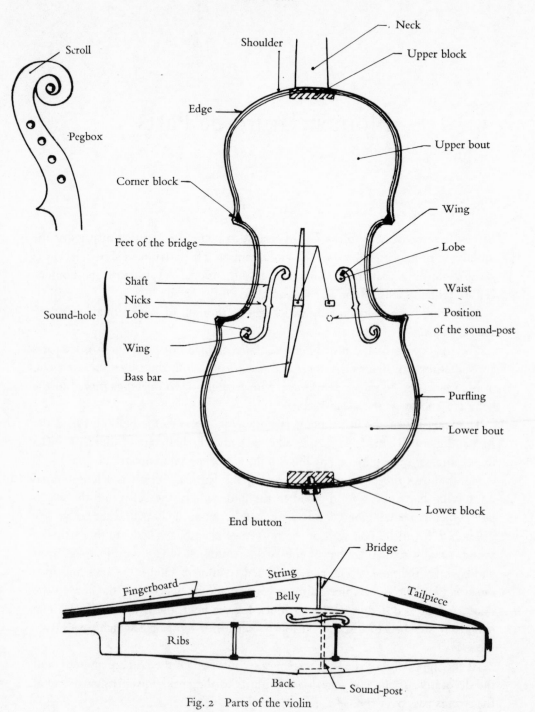

Scroll

Pegbox

Shoulder

Neck

Upper block

Edge

Upper bout

Corner block

Wing

Lobe

Feet of the bridge

Waist

Shaft

Nicks

Position
of the sound-post

Sound-hole

Lobe

Wing

Bass bar

Purfling

Lower bout

End button

Lower block

Bridge

Fingerboard

String

Tailpiece

Belly

Ribs

Back

Sound-post

Fig. 2   Parts of the violin

4

Origins of the Violin's Shape, and Some Curiosities of its History

The present shape of the violin is often taken for granted, almost as a God-given fact. There are those who believe that the C-shaped waist was brought about simply through the need for the bow to pass unimpeded over the outer strings; or again that the arching of the back and the belly arose primarily from the necessity for providing static resistance against the tension of the strings and the resulting pressure on the bridge.

It is possible that early violin-makers based their principles on the arithmetical proportions that exist between musical intervals. It is more likely still that they drew up their designs on the basis of particular laws such as that of the 'golden section'—a ratio used by the architects of Ancient Greece in finding the most suitable proportions for their finest buildings.

There are good reasons for the present shape of stringed instruments. Consciously or unconsciously, violin-makers were fulfilling an acoustical demand when they formed the waist using two C-shapes to dispense with unwanted sonority that would have been detrimental to fullness of tone, and carved out sound-holes in the form of *f*s.

The theoretical explanations are not simple ones. In this chapter we shall confine ourselves to a few points without recourse to diagrams, accepting it as axiomatic that violin-makers decided on the present geometry of the instrument's body after much experimentation and deliberation, a body representing an acoustical system whose form cannot be predicted using basic physical principles as the starting point.

When an incident sound wave is superposed on a sound wave that is reflected from a surface, so-called 'standing' or stationary waves are built up in the air, and these will vary considerably from one note to another. At some points in the air the incident and reflected waves just cancel, so that there is no resultant amplitude of motion or displacement of the air. This cancellation may occur at the same points at all times, and such points are called *nodes*. In a string the reflection from the bridge or any other stop will in general produce nodal points. In a three-dimensional cavity these will normally give surfaces called *nodal surfaces*.

The present shape of the instrument's body, with its arched belly and back, its C-shaped indentations in the central area and its *f*-shaped sound-holes, which break up the continuity of the grain in the belly, would seem to have the effect of eliminating, or at least considerably reducing, the detrimental effects that can arise from standing waves in the interior of the instrument. Experiments will show that these undesirable systems can be produced in, for instance, a round or ovoidal body as a consequence of such acoustically unsatisfactory interactions.

The sound-holes break up the continuity of the wood in the same direction as the grain, ensuring appreciable amplitude of the sound vibrations in those parts of the belly where they are needed for the production of certain notes, also acting so as to prevent their transference both across and along other parts of the belly.

The central ribs, which form an inward curve in the shape of a C, create a division between the two parts (upper and lower bouts) of the instrument. In this way both parts may be set in vibration virtually independently of each other; thus many effects which would be detrimental to the production and quality of the sound are eliminated.

The sound-holes, whose shape has an important bearing on the instrument's sound, also serve to link the air inside the instrument with that outside. And like the sound-holes, the central ribs too, with their C shape, have a further role to play: they reflect the vibrations of the enclosed air, at the same time avoiding any constriction of them, so that these too will produce the least possible number of effects detrimental to the instrument's sonority and timbre.

These considerations need not, however, lead us to believe that the great makers of the seventeenth and eighteenth centuries adhered slavishly to mathematical proportions or to those of the 'golden section' when they came to design and make their instruments. Their mastery, both as individuals and as a 'school', derived from lengthy experience with woods[1] taken from the same trunk, hence possessing identical properties. It was also the outcome of a particular form of applied acoustics: they would listen carefully to the various natural resonances of an instrument's belly and back and would bring them into harmony with each other. The belly and back would be hollowed out in such a way that they would yield the various resonances that the maker judged to be the right ones; by this means it was possible to obtain the desired sonority and timbre at the end of the next two stages, namely assembly and varnishing. It is in this aspect of their work in particular that the classic makers' high standards of artistry and craftsmanship as well as their fusion of taste with understanding can be appreciated. These qualities, of course, are gifts of nature, and training can only bring them into the light of day; but they could not have flourished without being favoured by the cultural, economic and artistic conditions of the times. Thus did the art of the great makers give us the shape of stringed instruments as we know it today.

To return to the subject of the origins of the violin's shape, it may be noted that quite recently the Russians—always to the fore in claiming priority for an invention—have announced[2] that an unknown painter 'probably' (?) of the late eleventh century, in a painting in the north tower of the Cathedral of St Sophia in Kiev, depicts a figure using a bow to play a stringed instrument, the latter being (even at that date!) held under the chin and against the shoulder. The physicist who made this announcement, G. Anfilov, states that this instrument very much resembles a violin. The bow, apparently, is already a straight one, whereas Western European bows of the time were still curved. (In Western Europe the straight bow is not pictorially represented until five centuries after this time.) The same writer—who, in addition to being a trained physicist, is also a popular scientific journalist—claims that without doubt the itinerant minstrels of Western Europe took their first stringed instruments from the Slavs.

Anfilov goes on to tell how in the towns of early medieval Russia musicians were persecuted by the feudal lords, and their instruments confiscated and taken outside the towns to be burnt. It is therefore not surprising, the argument runs, that Russian violin-makers were forced to emigrate and practise their art in Poland, France and Italy, slowly perfecting the instruments that were descended from the ancient Russian *gudok* (a three-stringed instrument known in the West as the 'rebec'); and it was in this way that the Polish *Geige* and ultimately the modern violin came into being. Such is the history now being published and taught in Russia, home of the great Oistrakh, Kogan and Rostropovich.

In other parts of Europe one has to go forward to the fifteenth century to discover the beginning of a more progressive shape in the violin, with arched belly. There is mention of a certain Kerlino who worked in Brittany and in Brescia (1450), and of a Dardelli in Mantua (*c.* 1500); we then come to Gasparo Diffenbrugger, who worked in Bologna from 1510 onwards. The instruments of these makers still appear somewhat primitive, but they reveal in embryonic form the shape that was to be evolved by Gasparo da Salò in Brescia. The latter's violins were already fine instruments, though still robust in appearance.

The great Norwegian violinist Ole Bull (1810–80) owned a Gasparo da Salò which possessed a powerful and masculine tone. He fell in love with the instrument after having seen and played it at the home of a Viennese collector, but it was not until long afterwards that he was able to acquire it in almost story-book fashion, and he played it constantly in concerts during his last years.

A pupil of Gasparo's, Maggini of Brescia, also made excellent instruments around 1600. Meanwhile, however, supremacy in the art of violin-making was passing over to Cremona where, during Gasparo's lifetime, Andrea Amati already had a flourishing workshop. It was in this workshop that a number of the most famous makers, including Stradivari and Guarneri, received their training before, in nearly every case, establishing their own workshops.

The instruments of the Amatis were pleasing in shape and, although not possessing especial strength of tone, had an excellent timbre. The decisive developments that were to bring the family of stringed instruments to their highest peak of perfection began with Nicolo, the teacher of Antonio Stradivari, who in turn set an example that was to be followed by every maker in Cremona with only rare exceptions such as Guarneri del Gesù, who sought out his own path. Every maker had his own entirely personal way of executing the finer details, but at that time the basic forms and concepts were for the most part taken over from Stradivari.

The figure of Antonio Stradivari[3] merits special attention. He worked in the Amatis' workshop as their pupil for a number of years. He began to sign his own violins in his twenties. When he set up on his own as an independent maker, he immediately began to experiment for himself. Progressive improvements led him to the so-called 'Amatisé' model, and later to the 'Longuet'. At the beginning of the eighteenth century. Stradivari, over fifty years of age, was at the height of his powers. All his genius was devoted to the construction of instruments that were perfect in every respect. (According to S. F. Sacconi, Stradivari was born in 1644 and died in 1737, as is clear from various labels authenticated as being in his hand. For instance, the violin known as the 'Venier', dating from 1732, is inscribed 'de anni 89', and in violins dating from 1733 we find 'de anni 90'. Stradivari even kept count of the months.)

Each of Stradivari's successive designs has sufficient breadth to yield a rich tone quality. Their contours are drawn with such taste and purity of line that even after 250 years they still delight violin-makers. He selected the finest woods and worked them with exquisite care. The arching is exemplary and gives his instruments a beautifully balanced sound that has never since been equalled. In order to realize what devotion Stradivari brought to his art, one has to look inside his violins. The most inconspicuous parts have all been made with quite exceptional care. The thickness he gave the belly and the back was determined in accordance with the properties of the wood and after mature deliberation: and the results always prove it to be entirely rational. All the different parts of the instrument are perfectly matched. Both the tone, which is full and mellow, and the timbre are of exceptional beauty. Courts, princes and cardinals asked Stradivari for instruments. In an era when transport, and hence information as well, moved at the speed of a horse-drawn carriage, his fame spread with incredible rapidity.

How may we imagine what this man was like at the time when he was producing his finest work? Polledro, leader of the Royal Orchestra in Turin, who died in 1850, relates[4] that his teacher had known Stradivari and remembered him as being tall and lean. At work he would wear a white leather apron and a white cap—of cotton in the summer and of wool in the winter; and since he was constantly working, his appearance never altered. He possessed remarkable balance of mind and body; any form of excess was foreign to his nature. His way of life enabled him to remain vigorous and active in extreme old age. Day by day Stradivari accumulated a wealth of experience stretching over some seventy years of working life.

His industry and frugality very soon made him a wealthy man; indeed, the inhabitants of Cremona used to say of a prosperous man that he was 'as rich as Stradivari'. He achieved this success in spite of charging only modest prices: his standard charge for a violin was four *luigi d'oro* (coins of that time such as florins and sequins would today be worth between twelve and seventeen Swiss gold francs). Consequently he was never short of work. It has been asserted that on his own he made two thousand instruments. This figure would seem to be too high, even taking into consideration the assistance he had from apprentices and from his two sons. Probably he made no more than eleven or twelve hundred instruments, as is stated by Hill and Sacconi (see Notes). This would mean an average of two every month during his fifty years as an independent maker. However, no more than about five hundred and fifty of his violins are known to have survived until now in usable condition, and of those made by Guarneri del Gesù the number is around a hundred and fifty.

5

Some Basic Principles of Physics and Acoustics

If a string or an elastic membrane is stretched between two fixed supports and set in vibration (Fig. 3), its vibrations will set up in the air a wave-like motion rather like the ripples produced when a stone is thrown into a pond. The *sound waves* produced in this way are formed by the propagation of vibrations emanating from the original string or membrane through the molecules of air. The mean position of the vibrating molecules of air remains unchanged; just as with ripples on a pond, what is transmitted is not matter itself but merely a disturbance. Air is an elastic medium, so that molecular vibrations occurring at any point in it will correspond to fluctuations in compression and decompression of the molecules themselves; there will therefore be constant fluctuations of density and pressure at the same point. At normal pressure and temperature (say 20°C/68°F) sound will be transmitted through air at a speed of about 350 metres per second.

In physical terms, a sound is an acoustical perception or sensation produced by vibrations in the air originating from the excitation of a sound source. A sound is

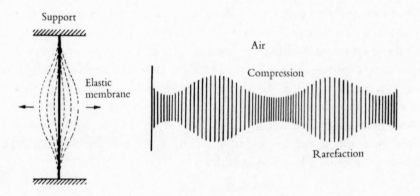

Fig. 3   Pulsations in air

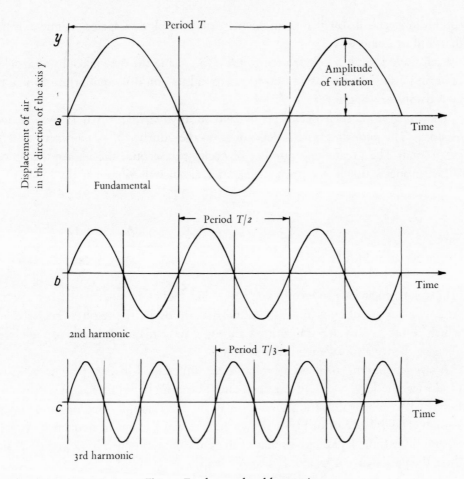

Fig. 4   Fundamental and harmonics

defined by its *pitch*, its *volume* (loudness or intensity) and its *timbre* (quality). As we shall see later on, its pitch is determined by the *frequency* of its vibrations, its volume by their *amplitude*, and its timbre by their *shape*.* In conventional terminology, a *musical sound* is one which represents a physical phenomenon of regular periodicity, whereas a 'noise' is a sound or complex of sounds arising from vibrations lacking regular periodicity and possibly of a confused nature. A *pure sound* is defined by a single frequency and the vibration that produces it is purely sinusoidal in form (Fig. 4, top): a particle of air oscillates around its point of

---

* See Chapter 6 for a more detailed analysis of sound.

equilibrium, and its oscillatory movement may be plotted against a time axis in the form of a sine wave.

Each wave form has a characteristic *period* (T), being the time taken by a particle of air in passing through every position around its point of equilibrium to make up a complete wave form.

The number of such cycles per second in any wave form is known as its *frequency*. The *pitch* of a note is dependent on the number of *vibrations* (or *cycles*) per second. The greater the number of cycles per second, the higher the note. When properly tuned, the open strings of a violin will vibrate at the following frequencies:

	E	A	D	G
Cycles per second (or Hertz)*	660	440	293	196

Lower frequencies produce lower notes, and higher frequencies higher notes. At a temperature of 20°C/68°F and at normal atmospheric pressure, the speed at which sound waves are transmitted through air remains constant for all frequencies, hence also for each different note.

A string vibrating to form a period T, as represented in Fig. 4 by wave *a*, is producing the lowest note it possibly can. This note is the *fundamental*. But the frequency at which the string vibrates may be, for example, two or three times as high. The lower part of Fig. 4 shows the sine wave forms of frequencies twice (*b*) and three times (*c*) as high as that of the fundamental which has a period T. In these the periods are $T/2$ and $T/3$ respectively.

Frequencies having periods $T/2$ or $T/3$ will yield respectively the *second* or the *third harmonic* (or *overtone*), giving a note an octave or a twelfth above the fundamental. There may be a large number of harmonics, and these, superposed on the fundamental, will determine the tonal quality of a note. When combined with its own harmonics, a fundamental will produce a *musical sound*, as distinct from the quite different effect of a pure sound.

In order for a solid body such as, for instance, a string, a rod or a membrane to be able to vibrate, it must possess a certain *mass* and a certain *elasticity*.

A wooden plank supported at each end, for example (see Fig. 5), is known to

---

* The Hertz (Hz), the basic unit for frequency in the International System of Units (SI), denotes one cycle or vibration per second. Thus a note with 660 vibrations per second is said to have a frequency of 660 Hz.

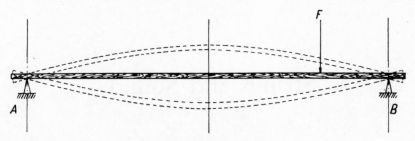

Fig. 5   Vibrating plank

possess its own natural period and consequently will vibrate at its own frequency. Both period and frequency depend wholly on the body's mass and elasticity, or, to be more exact, on the wood's *modulus* or *coefficient of elasticity*. This coefficient is defined as the ratio of stress to strain; the stress being the force per unit area (expressed as kilograms weight per square metre), and the strain the fractional increase in length which results from the applied stress.

If a momentary impulse is applied to the plank, it will be set in vibration. The *amplitude* of the vibration will depend on the strength of the impulse. (Amplitude is the maximum displacement from its mean position of the small volume of air through which a sound wave is passing.) If the plank continues to be subject to impulses at intervals which coincide exactly with its own frequency, it will vibrate with ever-increasing amplitude. When this happens, the vibrations are reinforced and we then say that the plank has begun to *resonate*. The regular repetition of dynamic impulses which, being synchronous with the plank's own frequency, reinforce rather than counteract each other ensures that full use is made of these impulses to achieve an effect in which there is a constant building-up of the amplitude of the plank's vibrations. The only limits to this effect are those set by secondary passive resistances such as friction occurring in the fibres of the wood, and damping by atmospheric resistance. It is when the vibration reaches its full amplitude, perfectly synchronous with the dynamic impulses, that full resonance results, and it is precisely this that is sought after in certain parts of the violin's belly, as we shall see.

6

Strings and Sounds

The production of gut strings is one of the oldest manufacturing processes in the world. Several thousand years ago primitive man was already making use of the entrails of animals. The first gut strings would certainly have been found on hunting bows long before man began to use them for musical instruments.

The string is one of the simplest of sound sources, and many physicists have used it as a basis for their studies in acoustics: notably Helmholtz and Bouasse, the latter the author of a classic treatise on strings and membranes.[1]

If a taut string is set in vibration—for instance, by a bow—a soft sound is produced. If the string is attached to a membrane or to a sheet of wood, then the sound will become stronger.

Nodes in sound have already been described in Chapter 4. On a vibrating string, they are the fixed points at either end and any other point along the length of the string at which the string does not vibrate; they are marked 'N' in Fig. 6. The points of maximum vibration (crests and troughs) are called *antinodes*; these are marked 'A' in Fig. 6.

As we have seen, sound is variable in *pitch*, in *intensity*, and in *timbre*, or quality. Intensity depends on the amplitude of the vibration of the sound waves; in fact, intensity is proportional to the square of this amplitude, so that if for example the amplitude of a wave is by some means doubled, the intensity increases fourfold.

The frequency or pitch of a string's vibrations can be increased by increasing the tension of the string, or by pressing it with the finger against the fingerboard so as to shorten its length.

The *pitch* of a note produced by a string will depend on the following:

the *length* of the string

its *tension*

its *linear density*, that is the mass of unit length of the string (measured in kilograms per metre).

34

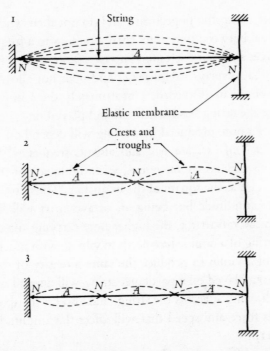

Fig. 6   Vibrating strings, showing nodes (N) and antinodes (A)

The *timbre* of the note depends on:

the nature of the string (fibrous or compact)

the mode in which it is bowed, struck or plucked, and in particular the point at which it is bowed, struck or plucked.

Any player is aware that it would be impossible simply to prescribe a given thickness for each of the strings of a violin. Only after trying out a large number of different strings is it possible to decide which gauge a particular instrument requires for each of its strings in order to produce its most satisfactory resonance. And to realize what influence the density and the material of the string have on its sound, one need only think of the difference in gauge and in tension between a steel and a gut string when the note E is played on the top string of a violin.

In listing the factors on which the production of a particular note depends, it was assumed that the string would possess the same thickness and density throughout its entire length. However, in gut and in wire-covered strings this is not always the case. Even the slightest irregularity in thickness and density along the length of a string will cause unevenness in its sound throughout its register. This deficiency will be obvious if two strings tuned in fifths are stopped by a finger at the same distance along the fingerboard and do not then when played produce a fifth. (The interval between two notes corresponding to a frequency ratio of 1 : 2 is called an octave, and that corresponding to a ratio of 2 : 3 is known as a fifth.) A faulty string that displays irregularities and does not allow the finger to slide easily along it should be discarded. Unfortunately these imperfections can only be detected once the string has been fitted and played on.

The *intensity* of a note produced by a string will depend on the thickness of the string, the *amplitude of its vibrations*, and also its frequency. Not only does the intensity of a note vary, as we have seen, with the square of the amplitude of the sound wave, but also as the square of the frequency. Thus, for example, two notes having the same amplitude but being an octave apart will have intensities (i.e. bear energies) in the ratio 1 : 4, the higher note carrying the greater energy. For this reason the string of a double bass needs to vibrate with much greater amplitude than the string of a violin to produce the same intensity of sound. The intensity of a particular note played on a particular string will depend on the force exerted on the bow in drawing it across the string, and also on the speed with which this is done. It is this force and speed that will affect the amplitude of the vibrations (see Fig. 7, A–A1).

As we shall see, different notes bring different parts of the belly into vibration. With the highest notes, it is the smaller masses that resonate. We have just seen that the higher the frequency, the higher the intensity associated with a given amplitude, and that we therefore hear the high-frequency vibrations of notes played on a violin as relatively loud. In addition, we must take into account the fact that sound waves of the same intensity but different frequencies do not draw the same aural response, as the ear tends to have its greatest response at relatively high frequencies, i.e. in precisely those registers most used in music. This is another area in which the master violin-makers displayed their artistry and technical ability to the full: only taste and faculties such as theirs could produce, in hollowing out the wood, such a fine balance between thickness and curvature of the belly and the back as to attain that marvellous evenness of sound on all the strings for which 'classic' instruments are so much admired.

We have stated that a vibrating string stretched between two points or stops will emit many other notes in addition to the fundamental. These other notes, i.e. *harmonics*, each have a frequency which may be found by multiplying the frequency of the fundamental by a single whole number. We shall not here go further into the technicalities of this matter.

Timbre, by which is meant what one might call the colour of a note and its beauty of sound, is dependent on the wealth of harmonics that accompany a fundamental, as Helmholtz demonstrated over a century ago.[2] It is from these harmonics that the ear can distinguish the sounds of two different instruments emitting a note of the same pitch and volume. For the physicist, timbre—again according to Helmholtz—is dependent on the harmonics present in a note. The resulting curve of a diagrammatic representation of a note will therefore vary from instrument to instrument, as Fig. 7 indicates. If the even-numbered harmonics are lacking or of poor quality, the result will be a rather nasal timbre

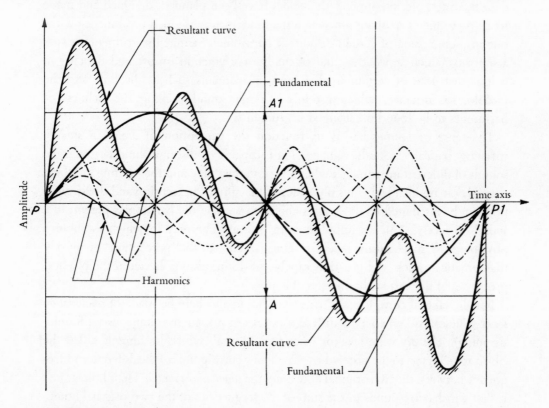

P - P1 · Vibration cycle

A - A1 · Amplitude of vibration.

Fig. 7 Harmonics

The fundamental oscillates as a perfect sine-wave. But since the amplitudes of the individual harmonics are added to that of the fundamental, a new resultant (broken curved line) is produced. For this reason a note which does not correspond to a sine-wave will have its own timbre corresponding to the resultant curve.

37

such as is characteristic of some Cremonese violins of the highest order; on the other hand, the presence of harmonics higher than the sixth renders the timbre astringent and hard, this being typical of many modern instruments. The production of harmonics is determined also by the material from which the string is made, by its gauge and by the manner in which it is set in vibration. In fact different harmonics will be produced according to whether the string is struck, plucked or bowed, and in the latter case the position of the bow on the string will also be a determining factor.

In the finest old instruments the bellies have been planned, designed and made so as to produce a resonance in which the fundamental is given prominence without any suppression of certain important harmonics. Stringed instruments possess a sonority which approaches that of the human voice in timbre and is richer in colour than that of certain smaller wind instruments such as the flute and the piccolo, for instance, which produce a purer sound, lacking the richness of harmonics to be found on stringed instruments.

The sense of *hearing* has as its function the perception of *acoustical stimuli*, meaning, basically, sounds. Our hearing is capable of distinguishing between the sounds of different instruments when the note they play and the volume at which they play it are identical. This physiological faculty of perception and discrimination can be attributed to the brain's ability to analyse the harmonics present in a sound on receiving nerve impulses from the ear. The way in which the brain's physiological mechanism reacts is comparable to the perception of purely mathematical ratios, and it is thus capable of distinguishing between the physical properties of the various harmonics of a note.

For the sake of completeness, mention should also here be made of *combination tones*. These arise when two different notes are played simultaneously (double-stopping). The *difference tone* (or 'suono di Tartini', which he himself called the 'third tone') refers to the note whose frequency corresponds to the difference in frequency between the two original notes; and the *summation tone* (or 'Helmholtz tone') is that which corresponds to the sum of the frequencies of the two original notes.

The *elasticity of the string* also has an effect on the harmonics produced and hence on the beauty and warmth of the overall timbre too.

If a bow is drawn with even force across a violin, the notes and harmonics will be more powerful in the low register, becoming weaker as the sounds move into the higher register. As already mentioned, however, our hearing makes compensations for this difference, as it is fortunately much more sensitive to higher frequencies.

Human hearing is at its greatest average sensitivity with notes in the region of 2,000 Hz, such as can be produced on the E string of a violin, for instance. Higher than this point of maximum sensitivity, there is a falling-off as frequency increases. Between a certain frequency and ultrasonic frequencies, the human ear is no longer able to perceive sounds. Both the lower limit (16–20 Hz) and the upper one (15,000–20,000 Hz) are of course subject to variation from one person to another, depending on the auditive faculties of the individual. Very young children and certain animals, such as dogs, can hear notes corresponding to a frequency as high as 20,000 Hz. However, the range of the human auditive faculties diminishes considerably as age increases: in general we can only hear notes which do not exceed 10,000 Hz in frequency.

What has just been said about the sensitivity of the human ear explains why harmonics have such a marked effect on the beauty, the colour and the fullness of an instrument's tone, despite the fact that they are of only moderate intensity.

It would be difficult to find two violins having the same richness and colour of sound. The amplitude of the various harmonics will vary from instrument to instrument; and since it is the proportions (i.e. relative amplitudes) of the various harmonics in a note that give the note its distinctive timbre, the timbre of each instrument will vary correspondingly.

The quantity and the precise combination of harmonics will depend on the type of instrument and its strings. A slender and elastic string will yield notes of extremely beautiful timbre; it will sound less well if played in a higher register, its length then being shortened. For this reason, stringed instruments give far greater scope for nuances of sonority than do small wind instruments, unless the latter are being played by a performer of outstanding artistry.

If a single note is played successively on each of the four strings of a stringed instrument,* we shall hear four different results, since each string will give an entirely different timbre, albeit at the same pitch. This gives the performer freedom to vary his timbre to suit either his own taste or the required interpretation. To the same end it is also possible to make use of the different possible ways of bowing and to vary the spot at which the bow meets the string. A further way of varying the timbre of a note is, as one is bowing, to bring the finger lightly against the string at a particular point rather than pressing it down, thus producing harmonics. The point at which the string is touched will correspond to the nodal point of the note one wishes to obtain.

* As, for instance, in Bazzini's 'Danza dei folletti'.

As we have seen, the timbre of a string depends on its elasticity, and that in turn depends on the material used, its length, its gauge and its density. Even though the thinner metal strings are more convenient and sometimes produce a very pleasant sound, they should not be used indiscriminately. The timbre of a gut string is very like that of the human voice. If, however, metal strings are fitted to a violin, a timbre is produced, especially on the third and fourth strings, which is very different from that of the human voice and not always pleasant. Its tone may perhaps be stronger but there is something artificial about it and it possesses less beauty. In former times, during the golden age of good taste in music, no-one would have dreamt of using a metal string in place of a gut one; its metallic tone would simply not have been tolerated. Nowadays, we must perforce put up with it. Metal strings are used by virtually all orchestral string players on grounds of cheapness and convenience.

It is said that Mozart was so sensitive that he could not bear the metallic sound of a trumpet. And when Paganini attempted to reinforce the effect of his violin by playing on thicker and more highly tensioned strings, the innovation scandalized his contemporaries, who described it as 'barbaric'. Paganini was compelled to abandon the idea very quickly. What would those contemporaries of his have said today, if they had been able to hear superb early cellos fitted entirely with steel strings, as frequently happens nowadays with Russian players? The use of metal strings should not be extended unthinkingly to such valuable instruments; exceptions may be made on grounds, for example, of greater reliability, but only for the E string of a violin.

Many performers, even the most celebrated, are unaware how much their listeners' judgement is influenced by the beauty of their instrument's tone, particularly when it is a question of comparing different gramophone recordings. I have often observed how music-lovers possessing particularly sensitive musical taste have found recordings made by famous quartets unsatisfying, and have preferred performances by less eminent groups simply because their sound was more pleasing. The microphone shows no mercy: generally it emphasizes the roughness of a metallic tone, instead of subduing it. The composer Giorgio Federico Ghedini, who disliked the sound of a cello fitted with steel strings, went so far as to be reluctant to write for the instrument through fear that his music would be performed on steel strings. He complained that cellos with steel strings sounded like 'packing cases', and he was quite right too.

Performers who remain loyal to metal strings ought to weigh up the pros and cons very seriously: it is certainly more convenient to use metal strings as they are stronger and cheaper, and require less frequent retuning; but they prevent the best sound from being obtained from an instrument. Many performers have overcome the taboos to abandon metal and have been thankful for it ever since.

We shall see presently how metal strings increase the pressure on the bridge, thereby putting excessive strain on the instrument, even to the point of making special adaptations necessary. Other kinds of adaptation have in the past resulted from the extension of the neck and the fingerboard made necessary both by the rise in real pitch of the principal note for the tuning of instruments, A above middle C, to 440 Hz, and by the exigencies of modern violin technique in which the higher notes and harmonics are used to a far greater extent than before. For the same reasons present-day violin-makers have been obliged to strengthen the bass bar too. The lengthening of the neck and the reinforcement of the bass bar have been the only modifications—and they are not material improvements—to which violin-makers of the nineteenth century felt obliged to subject the instruments of the old masters, which nonetheless, even after modification, to this day remain instruments we can look on as consummate works of art.

7

The Wood

In his treatise *Legni di risonanza*, written in 1918 for the *Proceedings of the Royal Florence Academy of Agricultural Sciences*, Piccioli refers to the 'wood from which the belly is made' as *Picea* (= pineaster), corresponding to the older vernacular term *pacera*. The normal Italian word for pine is *abete*, though previously *sapino*, derived from the French *sapin*, was used, and in some cases *abete-sapino* may be found.

The scientific name is *Pinus abies*, and more precisely *Abies pectinata* (silver fir) where the wood is white, *Picea excelsa* (spruce fir) where it is red. The use of pine wood in violin-making dates back a long time and is accounted for by its mechanical and acoustic properties which make it an outstanding transmitter of sound vibrations.

Volumes have been written about the use of pine wood by the violin-makers of eighteenth-century Cremona. Many writers assert that near the town there used to be a pine forest much valued by the violin-makers of the day, but which has now disappeared without a trace. Anyone familiar with the region will know how improbable this is. Others suppose that there used to be a special type of pine that has since become extinct. Both these hypotheses are extremely questionable. The best trees were those found in the Italian Alps in the regions of Trentino, Ampezzano and Cadore, where they still grow today at altitudes above 1,000 metres. Even the violin-makers of northern Europe used to prefer wood from these regions rather than, say, from Switzerland, Austria or Bohemia. The trees most in demand were those that grew under difficult natural conditions such as those on the southern slopes of the Alps. Geologically, the structure of the Alps is the result of a fault in the earth's crust, and their northern slopes are gentler and less precipitous than those towards the South. Consequently far more ravines were formed on the southern side and far more humus was washed away here too, leaving a thinner layer of soil. But poor soil promotes the growth of hardier and less resinous trees of the highest quality, whose wood dries more rapidly. In their search for the best pine wood, German violin-makers of the nineteenth century would go as far afield as the naval shipyard in Venice and the port of Fiume, where logs would arrive on rafts or simply floated in the sea.

Paganini liked to joke that Stradivari used only trees on which nightingales had sung day and night.

Documents show that in those days makers would buy pine trunks whole, frequently picking them out on the spot where they were growing. It is said that many violin-makers even made the trip to the high-lying valleys of Cadore in order to select trees on the basis of the resonant qualities they showed as they floated down-river. Nowadays it is virtually impossible to obtain a whole trunk and violin-makers have to be satisfied with sawn planks obtained from timber merchants.

Clearly it was a great advantage for the early makers to have an entire trunk at their disposal. It enabled them to gain a deeper knowledge of the mechanical and acoustic properties of wood, and hence to improve their craft from one instrument to the next. The uniformity of the woods used by Stradivari and other makers at different periods in their creative output is fascinatingly demonstrated by illustrations such as, for instance, those to be found in Hill,[1] Fridolin Hamma and Walter Hamma,[2] and H. K. Goodkind.[3] In these books, the instruments are shown in chronological order. The various periods in the makers' careers can be identified not only by differences in their typical working methods but also by associated differences in the woods they used.

In theory, pine wood of straight and regular grain ought to have been the most suitable for violin-making. But exceptions to this principle are legion. A first-rate pine unfortunately does not always yield the expected quality of tone. There exist superb old violins whose wood shows absolutely no regularity of grain, and certain famous violins display knots and structural irregularities that would scarcely be tolerated by a modern maker. The Cremonese masters would hoard a considerable quantity of wood from the same trunk in their workshops so that often there would be enough left over for their successors to benefit from. Their way of working with such a variable material as wood was masterly, even though they depended a good deal on pure intuition. They cannot have known that there is a difference between the speed of sound parallel to the grain and that at right angles to it. However, they must have known that the degree of flexibility of a plank cut with the grain running lengthwise differs from that of a plank whose grain runs crosswise.

Early in the nineteenth century, after numerous experiments, F. Savart[4] established that in pine wood the speed at which vibrations are propagated is four times greater along the grain than across it.

In the chapter on 'Varnish' we shall examine priming as a way of preparing the wood that was practised by the best eighteenth-century Cremonese makers. This process undoubtedly contributed to a kind of homogenization of the wood which we could almost describe as 'ossification'; this represented a major advantage, especially as far as the belly was concerned. It was not at all the same thing as the more general homogenization which Professor Koch of Dresden discussed in the journal *Umschau*.[5]

The violin-makers of the golden age were well versed in all the properties of the woods they used and knew about their finer points; they were quite happy to take sections from the best parts of the trunk even if from the purely aesthetic point of view these showed imperfections. For the bellies they could equally successfully use broad-grained pine or a harder, more closely-grained wood. They knew their materials so thoroughly that they could always choose the one they felt to be the most appropriate from the technical point of view.

Whereas pine wood has always been used for the belly, maple has tended to be preferred for the back. In Brescia, however, where Italian violin-making had its first beginnings, the earliest makers selected for their backs and for the ribs of their violas and cellos wood taken from the pear, ash and even the lemon-tree growing by Lake Garda. They knew how to combine these woods with pine of the highest quality in such a way as to give their instruments a gentle tone which carried well.

Later, above all in Lombardy, poplar or willow was used for backs. These woods imbued the violin with fullness and nobility of tone. There are also examples of instruments with backs of walnut, oak and beech, and still others, of the highest quality, using white poplar (*Popolus alba*). Nonetheless, maple gradually became the most favoured wood on account of its beauty and hardness. The decorative grain of this wood is the result of the tree's curious growth pattern; the grain takes the form of vertical 'waves' which are also intersected by horizontal rays (called 'curl' by the violin-maker) which marvellously reflect light. The beauty of maple wood is especially enhanced by the transparency of Cremonese and Venetian varnishes. The maple wood used in violins of the eighteenth century came from the Balkans as well as from Northern Italy. It appears that maple for violins was also taken from the blades of broken oars belonging to Venetian ships. These oars had been cunningly made from rather fragile wood by the Turks, who then maliciously delivered them to the Venetian Republic. At all events, maple from the Balkans had by then already become the most popular wood for making backs.

Thus on both aesthetic and acoustical grounds, pine and maple are the woods best suited for the various functions of the belly and the back as well as of the ribs, the neck and the scroll.

The violin-makers of Cremona used these woods almost exclusively; but they cut them in various ways. Building timber is normally sawn in slabs. For violin-making, quarter-cut wood is more usual (Fig. 8). In maple this emphasizes the attractive reflections mentioned above. Wood sawn in this way comes in wedge-shaped sections, two of which, when lined up and glued together, will form a 'flat roof' element from which a belly or a back may be cut with a minimum wastage of material.

Winter is the best season for felling trees from which wood for violins is to be taken: the sap should then have receded from the trunk and not yet begun to rise again. But nowadays, who could possibly be certain that the wood in the block he is being offered was taken from a tree felled in winter?

Apart from its properties of resonance, the most important qualities of a fine wood for violin-making are its *hardness*, its *elasticity* and its *resistance* to permanent distortion (a quality known in engineering terms as 'resilience'). All these qualities can be easily assessed and precisely measured by normal technical methods.

It cannot be over-stressed that it was primarily on acoustical grounds that the Italian masters chose their materials, even though the latter might not always

Slab-cut   Quarter-cut

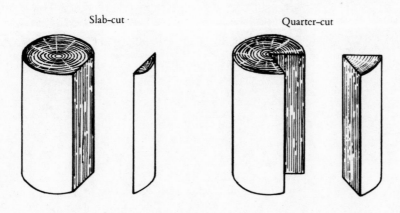

Fig. 8   Cuts of wood

have been the most visually attractive. Some of Stradivari's outstanding instruments, such as, for instance, the 'Alard', 'Berthier' and 'Hemming' violins and the 'Piatti' cello amongst others, contain small structural faults in the wood. Thus, in common with many of his contemporaries, this great master gave priority to the quality and reliability of the result rather than to the beauty of the wood. He did not reject blocks containing slight defects but worked them with great care and intelligence. In maple, broad curl and visual beauty do not always go hand in hand with purity of tone. There exist instruments of only moderate beauty which may nevertheless be accounted among the most successful from the acoustical point of view.

Concerning the drying of the wood, Bagatella is of the opinion that a good resinous pine will require at least three years.[6] An extremely important factor is the situation in which the tree grew, and also whether it was isolated or in a group of trees; in the latter case, again, whether it was on the outside or in the middle of the group. Trees that have been most exposed to the wind possess very much healthier wood because the fibres on the leeward side have been continuously subject to compression.

Methods of drying the wood need not detain us here. Systems of drying in ovens and processes of homogenization and impregnation with oleaginous substances, were all unknown to the violin-makers of former times.

8

The Body: Belly, Sound-Holes, Ribs and Back

If we examine the function of a stringed instrument from the acoustical and physical points of view, the *belly* will be seen as a special type of vibrating membrane that is partially held in check on its right-hand side by the sound-post and reinforced on the left by the bass bar. When notes of high pitch are emitted, the belly vibrates in a limited area on the right-hand side. With notes of low pitch the area of vibration is much more extensive and is for the most part situated on the left-hand side somewhat towards the centre. The belly represents a very specially shaped membrane which follows the peculiar contours of the ribs, and is irregular both in its thickness and in its convexities and concavities.

It is essential that the belly should possess in some area or other a good resonance for each of the instrument's various frequencies. In the finest classic instruments curvature and thickness are designed with such mastery that a marvellous uniformity of tone is obtained throughout the register. It would be impossible to say whether this is due to the technical knowledge, to the experience or to the intuitive abilities of the classic makers. The thickness of the belly will depend on the characteristics of the wood used—for instance, it will be greater in bellies of soft wood or in those with diagonal grain, so that qualities comparable to those of bellies made of harder wood or with vertical grain may be obtained.

To go into further detail here would be to risk becoming entangled in areas of discussion from which only the best violin-makers could extricate themselves. In constructing a belly the usual scientific calculations as used in construction work do not apply, precisely because of the peculiarities of the belly's shape and its variable thickness. The maker 'tests out' his block and hollows it out, using various tools. In this task he will use templates; but he will also be guided by the resonance itself, knowing what sort of sound the belly ought to give out.

Bellies that are thin and flat possess greater elasticity and consequently produce a better tone on notes in the middle and lower registers. In more steeply arched

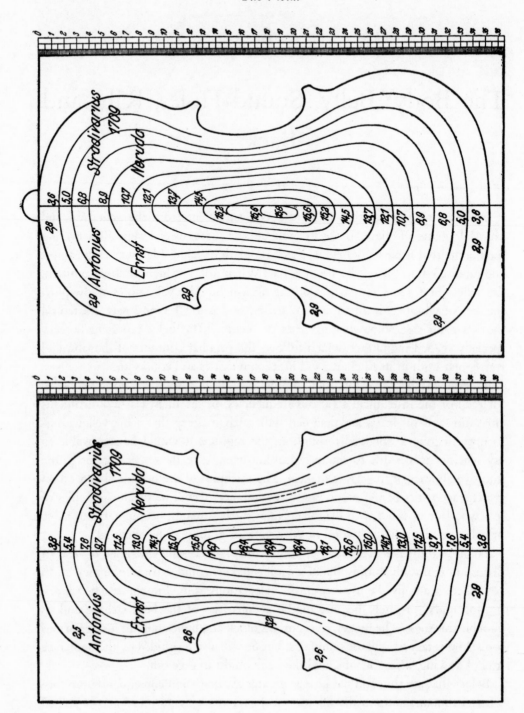

Fig. 9 Belly and back: contour lines (height in millimetres; scale on right hand side numbered in centimetres)

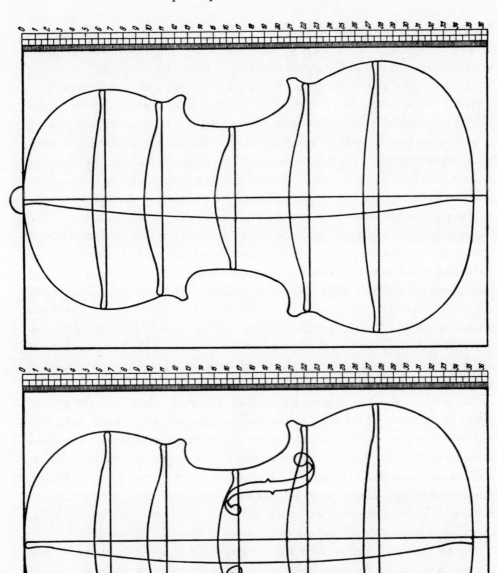

Fig. 10 Belly and back: curvatures of arching

bellies it is generally speaking the higher notes that sound better. The golden mean—in other words, the ideal compromise from the physical and acoustical points of view—is that which results in evenness of tone on all strings.

The belly must be elastic enough to sustain vibrations and at the same time it must not become deformed as a result of the static force imparted by the bridge (which rests on it). Here too there is no great mystery, as it is a question of striking a harmonious balance between a number of definable and measurable factors such as the characteristics of the wood, the shape, the thickness and the disposition of arching. It is here that the maker's artistry will be apparent. Figs. 9 and 10 show the contours of the arching on a 1709 Stradivari according to Nerudo.[1]

The purpose of the *purfling* is not simply to embellish the instrument. The violin-maker cuts a groove along the outer edge and fills it with three strips of service-tree or coloured pear wood. The strips are set into the belly alongside each other and glued down. In some very early violins the light strip is made of parchment, and similarly, dark strips made of ebony have been found. In northern countries violin-makers have even used whalebone. It is important that a material at once robust and flexible be used, since *the strips have to fulfil a mechanical function in protecting the belly*. In fact, the upper and lower edges of the belly are delicate and fragile; the purfling prevents serious damage in the event of the belly receiving a knock in the direction of the grain.

The purfling also has an *acoustical function*. The strips glued into the groove interrupt the wood of the belly so that the continuity of the material is broken and the active part of the belly—that in which the sound originates—is contained within a well-defined limit. As it vibrates, the belly sets in motion the air inside and outside the body. The *back*, which is not in direct contact with the bridge, is much more rigid than the belly because of its distinctive shape, its thickness, its mass, and the harder type of wood selected for it. It vibrates less than the belly, providing a resistance to the internal vibrations of air and reflecting them.

The air should be able to flow harmoniously out of and into the body; this purpose is served by the *sound-holes*, whose shape and position, including that of their nicks (as a guide for the correct positioning of the bridge on the belly), have a decisive effect on the quality of the instrument's tone. Each maker had his own solution to the problem of the shape and position of the sound-holes, these factors being crucial to the size and elasticity of the waist of the belly, as well as having a bearing on the vibrations of the upper and lower bouts and hence on the instrument's overall beauty of tone.

Various hypotheses have been put forward to account for the origins and present 'f' shape of the sound-holes. They became a feature of violins at the time of François I, and it was thought that they may have constituted a sort of homage to that king of France. But homage on whose part? Possibly that of Leonardo da Vinci, who, weary of the constant comparisons made between him and Michelangelo in Florence, had moved to France in answer to the summons of François I, remaining there from 1517 to 1519.

Universal genius that he was, Leonardo was also a fine musician. It is conceivable that he may have given his attention to stringed instruments and suggested to some violin-maker the shape of the sound-holes. This would have been no more than a token of his respect towards a protector and patron. However, it is highly improbable that he ever made such a distinctive contribution to the evolution of the violin. Leonardo noted down his projects and inventions in precise detail, copying the designs into his notebooks. In none of these (including those recently discovered in Madrid) do we find any suggestion of studies connected with violin-making.

The sound-holes are portions cut out of the belly giving its central part a degree of freedom and isolation from the outer parts of the waist; they enable the bridge to fulfil its percussive function more effectively. The most recent investigations and experiments concerning the effect of the sound-holes are those of Roussel.[2] He stresses the importance of their correct positioning, particularly that of the top lobe. In the opinion of this expert 'the top part of the sound-hole should not intersect a line running parallel to the instrument's axis from the extremity of the foot of the bridge, but should be situated close alongside it, so that the vibrating central area of the belly will not be excessively reduced. On the other hand, when the lobe is cut too far away from the said parallel, this area of the belly becomes less elastic.'

The curved shape of the rest of the hole too has its special importance. Where the shaft joining the top and bottom lobes is broad, there will be greater elasticity in that area of the belly where the vibrations occur; a narrower shaft has the opposite effect. Guarneri del Gesù carved narrow sound-holes, but elongated their shape. Stradivari preferred broader sound-holes. Both achieved outstanding results. And if their violins possess such characteristic differences in their timbre, this is in part due to the different forms of their sound-holes, since these determine the extent of the vibrating central surface of the belly.

The wings of the sound-holes vibrate above all in the higher registers, and they do so more through resonance than through direct excitation. In old instruments they possess a characteristic outline which in fact varies from one maker to another. Volumetrically, they display a special form with variable thickness, and their vibrations, together with those of the 'lips' or edges of the sound-holes, contribute to the vibrations of the air inside and outside the body, and hence to the production of sound.

The care violin-makers devoted to these minute details proves how important they were for them. But Roussel's interesting study of the shapes of sound-holes also contains an unfortunate proposal that the lower wings be removed, allowing the internal volumes of air to pass through to the outside of the instrument with greater ease. (The lower wings are of less importance to the formation of the sound than the upper ones.) If this modification were made, Roussel argues, the violin's sound would be more powerful and easier to produce. The timbre would indeed become brighter than that of the classic violins, but the tone would become comparatively harsh. What iconoclast would today have the temerity to perform such an operation on a fine old violin? Who would pay the price of renouncing the warm, rich sound of a golden-age Stradivari simply in order to obtain a questionable increase in power? For the present writer, power means a full and diffuse sonority differing hugely from that heard by the performer as he plays; a sonority which in the best instruments rises serene and limpid above the orchestra and, true as a sword, penetrates to the rearmost seats of a large concert hall.

The function of the *ribs* is primarily a mechanical one. They form an elastic connecting link between the belly and the back. Later we shall see how the belly expands and contracts as it vibrates. It is above all the upper ribs and those alongside the bass bar that must be sufficiently elastic to assist this action, and for this reason they were cut thin by the classic violin-makers, sometimes—as on Stradivari's instruments—being slightly bulged. Along the surfaces where the ribs join the belly and back they are reinforced by *linings*, strips of pine or willow which give a broader gluing surface. Looked at in section, their function is comparable to that of a blade held between two grooves. It is not hard to see why the lower ribs of old violins are much more robust than higher ones and those that are slightly bulged. The latter deform more easily and hence absorb less energy, but maintain tension in the belly less well so that the instrument loses some of its sinew. The heights of the ribs in old instruments were graduated so that they were lower near the neck of the instrument and higher at the tailpiece in order to give the desired ratio between the volumes of air in the upper and lower parts of the body.

For reasons of uniformity, the ribs in old instruments were made from the same maple as was used for the back, the neck and the scroll. The total volume of air contained in the body was determined by the average height of the ribs. Stradivari's cellos had very thin ribs, and as a precautionary measure he stuck strips of linen along the inside of them. (Subsequently there were makers sacrilegious enough to remove these and reinforce the ribs.) The ribs hold the belly, representing the vibrating membrane, at a precise distance from the back, whose principal acoustic function we shall presently see.

The maple used for the back must be hard so that the back can offer resistance without deformation against the force exerted by the static longitudinal tension of the body and by the vertical pressure of the sound-post. The fine varnishes of the old makers show off the regular, broad and elegant grain of the maple to good effect. As we have mentioned, the back vibrates less than the belly, and hence contributes less to the formation of the sound. The back reflects the vibrations of the air inside the body upwards towards the sound-holes; it functions like a reflecting wall, or a *repoussoir* as the Abbé Sibire picturesquely described it.[3]

The three elements we have described—the belly, the ribs and the back—were meticulously finished by the classic makers, using natural materials such as the skin of a young shark or a horse-tail, and then assembled and glued to form the sound-box. Many makers finished the surfaces when the body had already been assembled.

The belly and the back must be made acoustically compatible with great care. There are a number of ways of analysing their resonance and their natural frequencies. Undoubtedly the oldest way is to tap the block as it is being carved and hollowed. Fétis reports[4] that the method of rubbing the edges was thought of by Savart, and this too can be useful. In any case, before beginning their work, the Cremonese makers would assess the acoustical quality of their wood as an absolute value and make relative estimates of the desired ratio between the natural frequencies of the finished back and belly so that they could make the best possible sound-box. After conducting separate examinations of individual bellies and backs of Stradivari violins that he had at his disposal (those were the days!), Savart (*op. cit.*) came to the conclusion that the great master must have had a precise idea of how the tonal quality of an instrument depended on a particular ratio between the natural resonances of the belly and the back, a ratio that would be affected by their wood, its thickness and its curvature. A violin-maker can change the natural resonance and obtain the desired ratio by planing and scraping the wood away. The same author tells us that for Stradivari this ratio would be a major second (whole tone) or a minor third. He never relied exclusively on his intuition, but conducted experiments tirelessly, trying and testing again and again—in keeping with the motto of Galileo and of the Accademia del Cimento—in order to confirm the results he had obtained, to prove that the pitch of the natural resonance for the complete violin body occurs in the middle of the register in which the instrument is to function as a resonator.

The *sound-post* is a small cylindrical shaft of pine. The Italians call it *anima* and the French *âme* (both meaning 'soul'), whilst the Germans call it *Stimme* ('voice'). These various poetic names also actually define the sound-post's function. This small shaft is cut from a light, dry piece of pine with straight grain and should be perfectly cylindrical in form. The sound-post has a mechanical as well as an acoustical function. It has to help the belly to withstand the static force exerted by the strings on the bridge, as we have seen; at the same time it rests on the back and forms on the belly a nodal point for vibrations. The sound-post consequently has a considerable effect on the tonal quality of the instrument, on the one hand because of its physical characteristics and on the other hand by virtue of its position and the manner in which it is lightly wedged between the belly and the back close to the right foot of the bridge. Its correct position should be roughly along the axis of the right foot of the bridge and a little to the rear of it. It is up to the violin-maker to discover precisely the best possible position for it. This task requires instinctive flair, experience, patience and dexterity, and thus should always be left to a specialist. However, it would be wrong to imagine that an unsatisfactory instrument could be essentially improved by moving the sound-post; it is true that it is possible thus to make slight modifications to an instrument's timbre and sonority, but these qualities are principally dependent on other particulars which cannot be affected by the sound-post. Performers cannot be urged sufficiently strongly to avoid moving the sound-post themselves if it appears to be correctly positioned and the instrument sounds satisfactory. They would run the risk of injuring rather than improving their instrument's sonority.

The *bass bar* is another important component of the violin. It consists of a piece of fine-grained wood cut lengthwise and running underneath the left side of the belly along a line slightly oblique to the instrument's longitudinal axis and not quite parallel to the fourth string. The bass bar carries the vibrations passing through the left foot of the bridge, transmitting them predominantly to the left side of the belly, and because of its oblique position it affects a number of different grain-lines in that area of the wood. As with the sound-post, the bass bar, which is firmly glued to the belly, helps to resist static and dynamic forces, and the variable forces exerted by the bridge.

Like the sound-post the bass bar is carved from close-grained pine. Only an

Belly

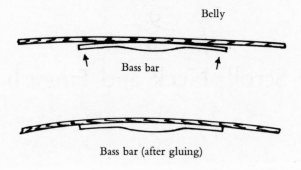

Bass bar

Bass bar (after gluing)

Fig. 11   Bass bar (section)

experienced violin-maker knows the shape and dimensions he must give it, as well as how and where it is best positioned; he will fit it according to the properties of the instrument in question, and will decide accordingly on its angle of inclination to the instrument's·axis. The bass bar supports the arched belly lengthwise, helping it to resist permanent deformation without adversely affecting its elasticity.

The bass bar is not carved precisely in accordance with the arching of the belly, but rather in such a way that, once it is glued on, it tenses the belly, and hence supports the arching too, as shown in Fig. 11. Its function is thus comparable with that of a scaffolding truss supporting the weight of a roof, or of a pre-stressed concrete beam built into a floor, and serving to keep it under tension and slightly arched. In time the wood of the bass bar may become weak or fatigued and the tension will be lessened. In such a case it is necessary to replace the bass bar, opening up the body of the instrument by removing the belly, an operation that requires great care and manual skill, and that can cause lasting damage if performed carelessly. An instrument will only be in perfect order if this operation has been carried out successfully.

9

The Scroll, Neck and Fingerboard

Up to the eighteenth century many violin-makers still adhered to an old tradition of decorating the neck of a viola or viola da gamba not with a scroll but with a carved head, perhaps of a blindfold woman, a sphinx, a cupid, or with the face of a Saracen or a bearded Philistine—and we may even find the head of a ram or of a lion. The violin-makers of Northern Europe continued this custom; thus the Tyrolean Jakob Stainer of Absam and Matthias Albani of Bolzano sometimes decorated the pegboxes of their violins with lion's heads. The great Italian violin-makers, on the other hand, kept their violins free from needless embellishment of this kind.

It may be of interest to read the opinion of Leopold Mozart (1719–87). In his famous treatise on violin technique, the father of Wolfgang Amadeus wrote:

At the extremity of the instrument, violin-makers lavish great ingenuity on bringing off a snail-like curve, or a lion's head. Indeed, they often attach greater importance to such ornamentation than to the main task of rational construction of an instrument. Consequently the violin—would you believe it!—falls victim to the deception of the world of appearances . . . He who values a bird by its plumage, a horse by its trappings, will also judge a violin by its decorative beauty and the colour of its varnish, without carefully examining its principal parts. So it is with all who judge by their eyes instead of their brains. But the beautifully carved lion's mane can improve the tone of the violin just as little as a majestic curling wig can improve the brain of its living wig-stand. In spite of this, however, many a violin is valued solely by such external trivia—and—oh dear!—how often does it happen that wealth, social position, and especially an imposing wig, is the authority that confers upon some turniphead the title of scholar, doctor or councillor?—But where have I got to? An excess of zeal against the common habit of judging by superficial appearance has led me quite astray.

Today the *scroll* is still often seen as a purely decorative element. The perfection of its form is in fact the maker's trademark. Who has not admired the scrolls of Stradivari? And yet, if one alters the weight of a scroll by a few grams, the instrument's power and timbre will be affected. This fact was known to the early violin-makers, and it is the belief of the present writer that they took account of it when they carved their scrolls.

Formerly, the scroll, pegbox and neck were cut from a single piece of maple, and the same piece of wood would be used for the ribs. Nowadays the scroll and pegbox of an old violin will almost invariably be grafted on because of the necessity of lengthening the neck (which we shall explain later). The *neck* is mortized to the instrument at the centre of the upper block.

To the neck is affixed the ebony *fingerboard*, and between this and the pegbox is attached the *top-nut*. To ensure the free vibration of the strings, they must be set at a specific distance from the fingerboard. This distance must not exceed certain limits if the instrument is to be played with ease. The neck is stuck to the body at a predetermined angle, so that the incline of the fingerboard, which in turn governs the height of the bridge, will allow the violin the conditions it requires for optimal performance. It is a known fact that the fullest sonority and the finest timbre can be achieved only when the static force that is transmitted from the string to the bridge and the belly matches the physical properties of the body as a whole.

A higher bridge will mean that the strings form a more acute angle and hence transmit a greater vertical component of static force to the belly. With a lower bridge, the reverse is true.

The best result is obtained by trying out different sizes of bridge and thus finding the most favourable height for the bridge after repeated experimentation. Another factor to be taken into account will be the characteristics of the violin body as a resonator. If the force exerted by the strings is too light, the instrument cannot have any fullness of tone. If the pressure is too great, it will become difficult to play, the sound will appear to be stifled, and the timbre will become unpleasant.

A point to remember here is that thin metal strings possess greater tension than gut strings when producing a note of the same pitch. The force bearing on the bridge becomes greater (and may even in fact be doubled!) and a fine old instrument may literally be stifled. The original sonority can often be recaptured by using a lower bridge on the violin and having only the E string made of steel.

If one wishes to play with a steel A string, the force exerted on the bridge can be reduced by using a suitable tuner to raise the point at which the string joins the tailpiece so that the angle at which it rests on the bridge becomes less acute.

The nineteenth-century practice of lengthening the original neck is another cause of excessive pressure on the bridge. Moreover, matters were made even worse by the higher pitch required by performers and orchestras, bringing the note A to a frequency of 440 Hz, since in order to produce this pitch, the longer strings needed greater tension. This lengthening of the violin's neck was a matter of approximately one centimetre, and arose from the necessity for greater ease of performance in the higher registers. It was furthermore thought that by lengthening the neck it would be possible to obtain a fuller sonority, provided that the instrument could stand the increased force bearing on the belly. It is said that Paganini would tune his instrument a semitone higher than the normal tuning. This can be explained by his desire for greater power of sonority from his violin, which was probably the famous Guarneri del Gesù instrument now preserved in Genoa. Having to play with an orchestra tuned a semitone lower would have presented no difficulties to that demonic virtuoso, and it is quite possible that his instrument—an extremely robust one—gained in sonority thereby (only gut strings being in use at the time).

10

The Varnish

No aspect of violin-making has provoked more discussion than the varnish used by the old makers. Specialists, non-specialists and speculators as well as serious violin-makers and researchers have tried to 'discover' its composition and in so doing to reveal the 'secret' of the superb varnish of Cremona or the gorgeous varnish of Venice.

A fine varnish is the most splendid ornament a violin can have. The varnishes of old instruments are especially enchanting, not on account of any patina of age, but because of the way they have worn. This unique effect is brought about by the colorations and shadings of long years of use. When such violins were new, their varnish had nothing like the same effect.

Does an old violin sound better today than it did when, fresh from the maker, it was coated with all its layers of varnish? Many old instruments have a splendid 'voice' and a marvellous timbre even though their body shows little more than mere traces of varnish. Often, indeed, only the first wash has survived.

Experts were given the opportunity of hearing two old violins from a museum. Both instruments were in a perfect state of preservation and their original varnish was completely unimpaired, as is the case, for example, with Stradivari's 'Messiah' violin. These experts observed that the sound of the instruments was inferior to that of other violins by the same makers whose varnish had been worn down by use. Other makers, equally expert in judgement, have maintained the contrary in similar circumstances. It is possible to suppose that superior sound obtainable from old violins that have been much played and whose varnish has been worn away may perhaps not be entirely attributable to the partial loss of the varnish; it may rather be that well preserved and seldom played instruments will not have acquired the correct and necessary degree of adjustment when examined by experts and for this reason do not possess the same quality of sound.

The great violin-maker S. F. Sacconi (Rome and New York), who repaired about three hundred Stradivari instruments and examined a further hundred or so of the roughly 550 instruments known to exist today, made extremely thorough and careful investigations throughout a life entirely devoted to violin-making. The results of his researches and the conclusions he drew from them seem to this writer to come closest to the actual facts of the matter. Although this book is primarily concerned with the physical functioning of stringed instruments, it seems important to give the essentials of Sacconi's views[1] concerning Stradivari's varnish and its effect on the sound of his instruments.

Stradivari made use of various mixtures in varnishing his instruments. He applied them to the body of the instrument in three separate stages of work. In the first place he primed and prepared the wood with a waterproof, transparent and shiny substance by coating all the outer surfaces of the instrument's body with it, using a swab. This priming also had the purpose of improving the mechanical properties of the wood. On the other hand, in order to harden and protect the wood on the inner surfaces of the instrument, he coated it with two layers of sheepskin gelatine (or parchment gelatine).

This *priming* represents a 'hardening and ossifying process, amounting almost to crystallization, which imbues the wood with a particular ability to vibrate'. After extensive research Sacconi came to this conclusion: the substance Stradivari used for his priming was potassium silicate (sometimes known as 'waterglass'). This substance renders wood more durable. It prevents the gradual decay of its fibres when subjected to the effects of vibrations in the course of performance, and ensures that the body will have a long life. In addition it allows thinner panels of wood to be used for the back and the belly because it homogenizes the wood, evening out its differing degrees of hardness. Even lengthy immersion in sea water has often left the wood unimpaired, as it has been possible to ascertain when valuable instruments have been salvaged from shipwrecks. It may be recalled that a misadventure of this kind befell the famous 'Trio di Trieste'. It was also possible to salvage the 'Mara' Stradivarius cello after shipwreck. The belly, ribs and back had been well insulated by Stradivari's priming. In contrast, an excellent Guadagnini violin disintegrated into so many pieces that it could not be saved. It may possibly have been in the water for longer; but it seems probable that that maker had varnished it by a different process.

The substance Stradivari used for priming his instruments takes on a 'warm cinnamon-like' tint when subject to oxidization. It insulates the wood from the varnish proper, not blending with the latter but marvellously reflecting its colour. Examination under the microscope has shown how this priming coat penetrated into the wood, clinging firmly to the pores without completely blocking them. When the varnish proper is applied it adheres to the priming coat and probably also grips those pores the latter has not entirely blocked.

The *varnish proper*—according to Sacconi—consists of *two different mixtures* which are swabbed on one after the other. There is no intermingling of the priming coat with the subsequent varnish, even by absorption, because Stradivari applied a white insulating substance on top of the priming coat. This consisted of albumen, gum arabic and honey. The difference between this process of priming and varnishing as it was practised in Stradivari's day and what is (with some exceptions) usual today is to be found in the different layers, their composition and their manner of application.

Stradivari applied the coloured varnish not with a swab but with a brush. It is very sensitive to heat, and Stradivari was afraid of cracks developing, particularly during the hot Cremonese summers. This outer varnish is elastic and supple, but at the same time very susceptible to knocks; traces of splintering can often be found, particularly on the back.

Among other things, the varnish contains *propolis*, a resinoid vegetable substance used by bees to block up pores and fissures in their hives and also to attach honeycombs to them and, indeed, 'varnish' them. It is this substance that gives the varnish its golden amber tint. The propolis was mixed with resin of larch turpentine (also known as Venetian resin) as a binding agent and with oil of turpentine as a solvent. In order to give the varnish greater or lesser coloration, a non-soluble ruby pigment was added whose particles would consequently remain suspended in the varnish. It is thought that never were more than three layers of this varnish applied, and they were always laid on with a brush. After this procedure came the burnishing and polishing of the surfaces.

The other fine violin-makers of Cremona also practised a method comparable to that of Stradivari, as had the famous earlier intarsia workers of that town; examples of their work can still be seen today in Cremona.[2]

Such an infinity of words has been written about varnish in general and coloured varnish in particular that it is extremely difficult for a layman to know where to turn for information. For this reason the reader wishing to pursue the subject further is referred to the chapter on varnishes in the book by Sacconi already cited.

It is hard to understand how at the end of the eighteenth and the beginning of the nineteenth centuries—that is, after the time of G. B. Guadagnini and Ceruti, who may be considered the last of the Cremonese makers—the famous so-called 'formula' and the method of applying the varnish came to be forgotten. It is the present writer's view that this was due to a process of decline in violin-making. It would also seem that the violin-makers of the nineteenth century possessed less musical sensitivity than their predecessors; in addition they lacked knowledge about the effects of varnish on tonal quality. Neither should we forget what great changes had gradually been brought about with the passage of time. Gone was the age of courts, princes and cardinals, and with it the days of relatively well-paid commissioned work. In such circumstances violin-makers sought to make economies. Their smaller profits induced them to buy less costly varnishes which demanded less time and care in their application and dried more rapidly. Such considerations may already have carried weight with Guarneri del Gesù, whose abilities were comparable to those of Stradivari. During his lifetime his talents were not sufficiently appreciated, perhaps even on account of his varnishes, which were often not so fine as Stradivari's. It was only long after his death that his genius was recognized. Cozio di Salabue wrote of Guarneri del Gesù in his memoirs (1816): 'Twenty years after his death it was possible to buy a job lot of his violins at two or three sequins each.'[3] After this maker, the true decline of fine varnishes set in. They had lost their incredible transparency and their magnificent play of colours. Quality became constantly worse, and often varnishes were even cloudy.

Sacconi concerned himself above all else with the problem of varnish because he found it hard to understand why no research, even including that undertaken on a serious basis, had yielded any usable results. It was probably thought in his time that the composition of old varnish could be reconstructed by going back in time and studying old writings and recipes, even though these unfortunately had little to do with violin-making. This compound was subjected to precise scientific analysis by later researchers (a difficult undertaking, since, in view of the priceless value of the material, analyses had to be conducted using only the tiniest fragments). Yet when it came to the question of actually reconstructing the composition of individual varnishes, even these researchers could not provide an answer, since they still had no way of knowing what the constituents of each of the various layers of varnish were.

For many violin-makers the subject of varnish became a somewhat disagreeable problem in the course of time. Varnish almost came to be considered a 'necessary evil', indispensable for keeping the wood in a good state of preservation against the player's sweat and atmospheric effects as well as for embellishing the instrument. 'Even the finest and most suitable varnish cannot improve the original sound of a violin; at best it can only degrade it,' wrote Droegemeyer at the beginning of this century, having established that a violin possesses a more powerful sound before it has been varnished.[4]

The sound of a 'white' violin (as makers call them) is certainly more powerful than that of a varnished one, but it is less pleasant and harsher. (It is only possible of course, to conduct such tests with modern violins.) Fortunately Droegemeyer's pessimistic conclusion has proved incorrect, especially where old instruments are concerned. In 1937 Meinel published a study of the violin's acoustical frequency spectra using the resources of modern scientific technology.[5] He established the fact that a good modern artificial varnish would tend to produce a flattened frequency spectrum, dampening the maxima and minima, particularly at higher frequencies. This is beneficial to the sonority since it is precisely in the higher frequency range that the tone of a modern violin will often seem somewhat harsh and its timbre less warm. The damping effect by which maximum and minimum values in the frequency spectrum are levelled out has the additional advantage of allowing the fundamentals to emerge more prominently (Fig. 12).

Let us now return to our physical and acoustical observations. The mass of the belly is slightly increased by the addition of layers of varnish, but at the same time there is also a change in its coefficient of elasticity (see Chapter 5). If the priming coat is applied according to Stradivari's method, the wood will 'ossify' and the coefficient of elasticity will be more favourable still. However, an increase in mass will also bring about a decrease in the belly's natural frequency.

In general terms, priming and varnishing will make the elasticity of the wood

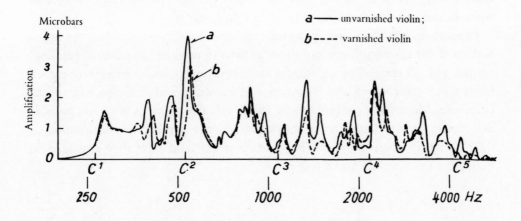

Fig. 12 Frequency spectra before and after the application of varnish (according to Meinel)

more uniform and improve the instrument's timbre. And, again if we are referring to old instruments, it is undeniable that varnish, fullness of sonority and timbre are very closely interrelated. Of course, this fact should not be given exaggerated importance. If the priming and varnish of Stradivari and the other Cremonese masters were exclusively responsible for their instruments' tone quality, then their predominant feature would be a total uniformity of sound, and this is not true of the finest violins by the great makers. Their products are always strikingly individual.

S. F. Sacconi (*op. cit.*) could base his findings on what was, statistically speaking, a vast experience of the subject, since he was able to conduct experiments on countless instruments displaying varying quantities of varnish. He confirmed what observation would lead one to believe: it is not the coloured varnish that has such a favourable effect on the instrument's sound, giving it what is known as the 'Italian' timbre, but rather the priming coat, which renders the wood extremely hard and resistant, even after the coloured varnish has been removed. When it has been primed the wood ossifies and becomes extremely *elastic* and resistant. Because of this, Stradivari was able to give his bellies and backs the thinness which violin-makers consider to be the best for producing a timbre both powerful and beautiful, if also darker than that of instruments with thicker bellies.

In contrast, the effect of the coloured varnish is insignificant. The small quantities that can be applied with a brush and the delicacy of the resultant layers can hardly significantly increase the mass of the part in question. For this reason, violins bearing only traces of varnish can also sound perfect—perhaps as beautiful or more so than when they still had nearly all their varnish.

Experience, tradition and peaceful working conditions enabled the great makers of the eighteenth century to judge what would be the effect of priming, varnish and the method of application on an instrument whose parts were carved from a particular wood and possessed a given shape and thickness and special curvatures. Varnishing provided them with a valuable aid in evening out possible deficiencies or tiny faults in the instrument. Hence it made its contribution to their extraordinary success and helps us to understand how they managed to transform a noble craft into a true art.

II

The Bow

It is no easy matter to choose the right bow. The correct choice involves bringing the 'trio' formed by performer, instrument and bow into tune with each other. The bow is indeed a delicate and unique element, whilst the performers who use it are totally different from each other. They all have their own special biological and morphological features, likewise each is endowed with a different temperament.

Bow and performer must therefore possess suitably complementary qualities in order for a particular instrument to achieve its best sonority. A bow may also be more, or less suitable for playing a specific kind of music, given an identical performer and violin. For example, a bow with a heavy head is eminently suited to *cavata* playing but less appropriate for *saltellato*.

The characteristic properties of a bow are: its *weight*, the position of its *centre of gravity*, the *shape* and *mass of its head*, and the *elasticity* and resistance to permanent deformation of its wood.

As far as the shape is concerned, the bow stick should be absolutely straight along its vertical plane, it should taper towards the head with a certain regularity determined by the bow-maker, and it should offer elastic resistance to bending in both its vertical and its longitudinal planes.

The *hair*, consisting of between 175 and 200 horsehairs, must be selected with great care. The best hairs are white and of moderate thickness. If the hairs are too thin they will break easily, and if they are too thick they will exhibit insufficient roughness and rosin will not adhere well enough to them. The weight and thickness of the hair must be suited to the bow as well as to the requirements of the performer. According to Roussel (*op. cit.*), a good individual hair must be able to sustain a tension of some 0.3 kilograms weight and stretch 20 per cent of its own length before snapping.

It is not necessary here to go very deeply into further details. Every maker of bows and every performer will have his own experience of the matter, and will have formed his own personal views.

Rosin is needed for good, regular friction to be produced between the hair of the bow and the string. Its alternative name, 'colophony', originates from the name of a town in Asia Minor from which rosin was at one time obtained. It is a resinoid substance obtained from maritime pines and cedars. It fulfils an important role, for upon its composition depends the bow's coefficient of friction against the strings, which in turn, as they vibrate with greater or less force, bring the entire instrument into resonance.

Each performer has his own requirements and his own individual sensibilities. He will correspondingly choose from among the various types of rosin the one he finds most suitable. It may be bright, dark, relatively powdery or less so. A violinist playing before a microphone will prefer a soft rosin, whereas in a large concert hall with full orchestra he will use one that gives more bite to his bowing. He must never forget carefully to wipe down the bowstick and the instrument itself after playing since rosin dust will adhere to the varnish, especially when the latter is of a delicate kind. If not regularly cleaned off after use, this dust can form an ugly black crust which may even affect the instrument's sonority.

The *bow-maker* must possess ability of both a craftsmanlike and an artistic order. He must know how to work with hard wood, such as, for instance, Pernambuco, Brazil and ebony; he must be able to handle ivory, tortoiseshell and mother of pearl. In addition he must possess skill in metal-turning and know how to work and solder various alloys of gold and silver.

The great exemplars still remain the French makers of the last century. They were unrivalled in their choice of woods, as in the beauty and the quality of their work. Tourte the Younger (1747–1835) used Pernambuco wood, excellent for keeping its shape and for lightness. It could be obtained in France without difficulty, being taken from the staves of the sugar casks coming from the colonies at that time. Numerous French and German contemporaries of Tourte followed his example. It was as a consequence of this innovation that the makers of the time were able to produce perfect bows which today are sought out as masterpieces. It was also Tourte the Younger who established the precise lengths of bows: 75 centimetres for violins, 74 centimetres for violas and 74 centimetres for cellos.

How Stringed Instruments Function

If a bow is placed on a string and drawn across it, the latter is pulled sideways between its point of rest A (Fig. 13) and a second point B, and the force of recoil arising from this lateral stretching of the string will become greater than the starting friction between the rosined hairs of the bow and the string being played. Freeing itself from the hairs, the string returns with a higher velocity through point A towards point C; at this point the hairs of the bow will repeatedly pick it up again, but as often as they do so the string will again free itself, producing vibrations. These vibrations have special characteristics, and physicists call them 'relaxation oscillations'. They have the useful property of being rich in harmonics.

Fig. 14 shows a diagram of these vibrations as plotted against co-ordinates of amplitude and time. These vibrations are acoustically perceived as if they resembled sine waves, though this is not at all the case. Their cycle corresponds to

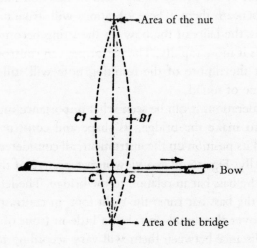

Fig. 13   Bow

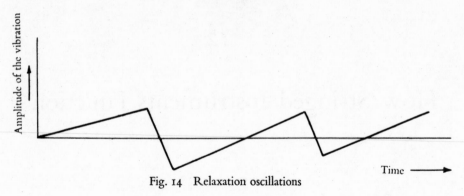

Fig. 14   Relaxation oscillations

the number of vibrations of the fundamental—in other words, of the deepest note the string is capable of emitting. As has already been pointed out, harmonics (for instance from the third to the fifth harmonic) are superimposed on this. If a graphic representation of the result of adding the amplitudes of the harmonics to those of the fundamental is drawn, something like the diagram in Fig. 7 will be obtained, in other words, a cyclically recurring sine wave distorted by the super-imposition of additional peaks and troughs.

The string's oscillations are transversal to the bridge, transmitting to that elastic system vibrations which are in turn transferred to the belly. The feet of the bridge can for the most part vibrate only in a plane perpendicular to the belly (Fig. 15) and will cause a part of it to resonate. The evenly balanced alternating vibrations of the feet of the bridge cause them to function like rapid percussion drills on the belly beneath them. These vibrations will strike more powerfully as the force exerted by the hairs of the bow on the string becomes greater and the bow is drawn across it more rapidly. The performer can control these two factors in such a way that the timbre of the resulting note will still remain agreeable whatever the volume of sound.

From these considerations it can be seen what importance must be accorded to the material used to make the bridge, its shape and construction, the distance between its feet and its position on the instrument, all considered in relation to the properties of the belly. Fig. 16 gives a view in perspective of the positions of the sound-post and of the bass bar in relation to the bridge. The left foot rests on the belly above where the bass bar runs; the right foot, in contrast, does not rest on the belly precisely over the sound-post, but a little in front of it, though still in line with it. (The distance between them will vary according to the thickness of the belly.) This arrangement represents an ingenious solution permitting the belly to be set in vibration on high notes in the most efficient possible way.

It is the strings playing in the higher register that chiefly activate the percussive function of the right foot of the bridge. Conversely the strings playing in the lower register are those which chiefly affect the left foot and thereby also the area of the bass bar, as we shall presently see. The sound-post, which is lightly wedged between the belly and the back, forms a 'nodal point' on the belly for its vibrations. It may be thought of as a free-standing upright with a lintel-like structure to support.

The instrument, seen as a whole, is then a wooden, elastic assemblage with a very individually shaped resonance chamber. It consists of horizontal elements which are arched and have differing thicknesses, and vertical elements adapted to the special horizontal contours. All these elements are stuck together and form, in physical terms, a 'resonance chamber' or 'resonator'. Its task is to increase the acoustic power of the instrument by reinforcing the fundamentals of all its notes as well as their corresponding harmonics. The belly vibrates under the regularly alternating percussion of the feet and in the same rhythm with them. As it vibrates the upper hump of the belly is deformed for a while on the right-hand side, where the sound-post is situated, in a different manner from on its left-hand side where the bass bar is attached. Likewise different vibrations and deformations occur in the two lower areas on the right and on the left, because the vibrations emanat-

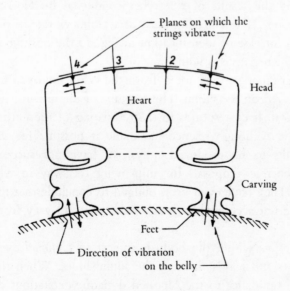

Fig. 15   Bridge

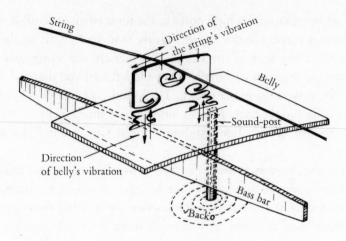

Fig. 16   Position of bridge, sound-post and bass bar

ing from the hump of the belly across the central zone bounded by the sound-holes reach the lower areas of the belly by way of an asymmetrical system (sound-post—bass bar). Thus the four sectors of the belly all vibrate in an independent manner that is quite different from one to another. The accuracy of this description is borne out by the results of researches conducted by H. Backhaus and G. Weymann (Fig. 17). The vibrating areas of a violin vibrate in opposite phase to each other, and for ease of identification in Fig. 17 the positive areas are shown as shaded and the negative as white.

For this experiment various notes, from the G on the open fourth string upwards, were played on the violin. The response of the instrument at a frequency of 274 Hz is ideal. It corresponds to the resonating of the entire volume of air inside the body. Although science has made it possible for such precise and significant results to be produced, physicists have not succeeded in finding formulae or concrete proposals for improving the way in which violins are actually made. They have even been obliged to conclude that these phenomena of vibration are not accountable to any rules and will vary from one violin to another.

The *volume of air* within the body is subject to *continual compression and expansion*. It enters and leaves through the sound-holes. When the body gives a relatively good resonance to the repeated dynamic excitations of the belly and the internal pulsations of the volume of air, this will have a beneficial effect on the instrument's tonal power, enhancing its colour and brilliance.

For the physicist a machine is no more than an apparatus designed to perform work: it transforms an input of energy into a different form of energy, as for instance mechanical into acoustical. Thus a stringed instrument is no more than a machine for transforming the mechanical energy of the performer into the acoustical energy of sound. As has already been said, the essential part of this machine is a very special apparatus known as a *resonator*.[1] Only a little of the mechanical energy it transforms through the friction of the bow on the strings gets wasted in producing heat. Because of its excellent efficiency, therefore, a stringed instrument is an almost perfect machine. The instrument's quality will depend on its acoustical capacity. From the scientific point of view, its body possesses an indeterminate structure—in other words, it is extremely complex since it represents a structural system containing many restraints. The calculation of stresses in indeterminate systems is beyond the methods of basic mechanics, and can be done only by taking account of elastic deformation—a task difficult enough, in the context of large-scale metal frameworks, usually to be performed by computer. We may confidently say that the attempt to measure the forces that operate in a violin's body, with all the elastic deformation such a body is subject to, would hardly be within the practical bounds of any research budget.

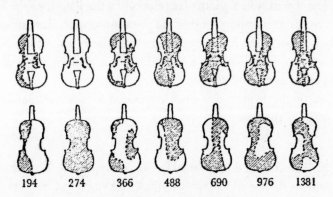

194   274   366   488   690   976   1381

Frequencies in cycles per second (Hz)

Fig. 17   Zones of vibration in the resonance chamber (belly and
back)

Positive (shaded) and negative (white) zones of vibration for a
series of notes whose fundamentals range from frequencies of 194
Hz to 1,381 Hz. The frequency 274 Hz corresponds to the natural
resonance of the body (after H. Backhaus and G. Weymann)

71

13

Towards a Theory of the Bridge

Today the bridge (see Fig. 15) still keeps to the shape Stradivari used. Violin-makers used to have to carve all their own bridges from planks or tree trunks; nowadays dealers will supply them ready cut to size, ready to be finished in detail. The wood used is nearly always maple, which must be hard and well-seasoned.

Seen from the point of view of statics the bridge functions as an upright of variable cross-section, unequally supported from above and below. It takes the force exerted by the strings and rests on the belly with its two feet, whose soles must be precisely matched to the belly's curvature. The exact position of the bridge will be determined by the instrument-maker with the aid of the nicks in the sound-holes; it stands in a particular relation to the length of the belly and its other characteristics. It is important that the point of support thus indicated should be scrupulously respected as it must coincide with the centre of the belly's vibrations, as already established by the maker. Incorrect positioning will restrict the instrument's performance and timbre.

The function of the bridge was once explained in a somewhat confused but imaginative way by the nineteenth-century violin-maker Haweis:[1] 'The bridge,' he wrote,

has not only the important and indispensable task of supporting the four strings which exert on it a combined force of 70 pounds (about 30 kilograms), but is in the most in-timate contact with the rest of the violin—more so than any of its other parts. It rests on the wood, or rather is pressed against it almost to the point of being forced into it, so that it forms a far closer link with the instrument than the fingerboard, the tailpiece or even the corners and corner blocks. On the one hand it is charged with the vibrations of the strings and on the other hand with those of the belly, the ribs and the back. Within that marvellous column of vibrating air contained inside the walls of the violin, nothing can happen of which the bridge is unaware, whether it assists or hinders the escaping sound waves. I must admit that at first I held somewhat fanciful views about

72

the bridge; however, many years of experience have convinced me that it is not easy to procure a bridge that is completely suited to a violin; and it is really rather foolhardy to make light of the intimate, as it were *marital* relations between bridge and violin.

When we considered questions of mechanical acoustics and the way in which a stringed instrument works, we saw that the function of the bridge consists in imparting to the belly the vibrations of the strings arising on planes whose envelope corresponds to the curvature of the bridge itself (see Fig. 15). The vibrations are transmitted to the belly with the help of the feet which function like small hammers in a direction almost perpendicular to the strings ('The tremolo transmitted to it by the bridge.'—*Memoirs* of Count Cozio di Salabue.) This kind of transmitter of mechanical energy must satisfy many requirements: it must not absorb too much energy itself, because an excessive elasticity would benefit the lower notes at the expense of the higher ones, which would then become weaker. On the other hand, it should not be too rigid, because then the higher notes would predominate.

Here too it is part of the violin-maker's art to find an ideal compromise not only in taking into consideration the thickness of the wood but also in finding the right proportions for the incisions and matching the soles of the feet exactly to the curvature of the belly. The heart-shaped carving and the lateral indentations, which reduce the active part of the wood between the head and the feet, as also the form of the feet themselves, are not merely decorative, but have the important task of giving the bridge the right degree of elasticity. Every instrument requires its special bridge, of suitable shape, hardness, thickness and elasticity.

As yet there exists no complete 'theory of the bridge'. For this reason we shall now have to concern ourselves with a number of theoretical considerations, as this component has an important bearing on the instrument's potential acoustical performance.

The feet of a bridge must be of a particular height and at a particular distance from each other in order to be able to fulfil their function. The vibrations of a string take place on a plane virtually parallel to the belly, so that the latter is activated primarily in a transverse direction. A piece of wood having neither carved-out sections nor feet, its entire width being in contact with the belly, would produce a far weaker tone, the belly being able to vibrate only to a limited extent (see Fig. 18a).

Let us now take a look at a bridge that has not been carved out and has been stuck onto a homogeneous flat belly—without arching—of constant thickness. If

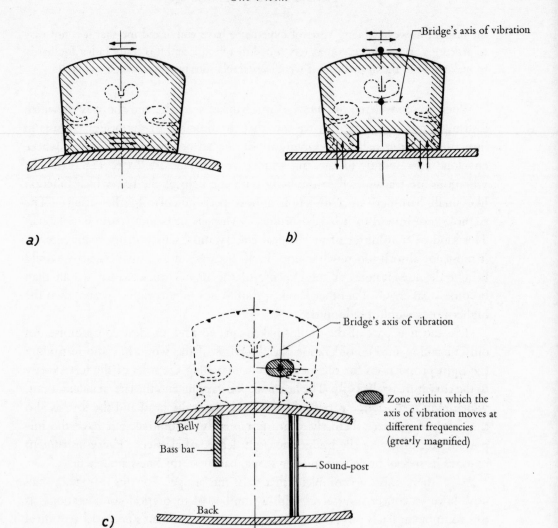

Fig. 18   Three different bridges

a)   The belly vibrates very slightly
b)   The feet vibrate with equal intensity on a level, symmetrical belly
c)   The bridge's axis of vibration at typical frequencies

we disregard the dynamic asymmetry arising as a result of the friction of the bow on the different strings, the bridge will oscillate in its own plane, i.e. turning at certain angles. The angular vibrations will occur around an axis situated on the vertical central plane—an axis perpendicular to the bridge and equidistant from the feet. However, since the bridge is also symmetrical the feet will vibrate with the same intensity (see Fig. 18b). But because of the presence on stringed instruments of the bass bar and the sound-post wedged in position to the right of it (see Fig. 18c), we must look for the bridge's *axis of vibration* in an off-centre position. It is hard to say exactly where this position will be. Nevertheless, the above reasoning can lead to a fair approximation.

The right foot allows the belly to vibrate with less amplitude than the left, because it rests on it only a few millimetres away from the sound-post, and the back of the instrument is less elastic than the belly. Thus the sound-post damps and limits the amplitude of the vibrations on the upper right-hand side of the belly.

In contrast, the left foot, which rests on the belly above the bass bar, is in a better situation. The vibrations it transmits to the belly can be of greater intensity. They also have a lower frequency, since they mostly come from the instrument's lower-register strings. Thus the two feet vibrate in a different way from each other. Hence it is obvious that the bridge's axis of vibration is to be found neither on the vertical plane of one of the feet nor at any point symmetrical to the feet. On the contrary, we must look for it in a limited area between the vertical plane of the centre of symmetry itself and that which passes through the foot that is less free to vibrate, namely the right foot.

The precise position of this axis of vibration at any given moment can therefore be determined only for a single frequency, hence a particular note, on a given bridge mounted on a particular instrument. But if the instrument is played so as to produce a number of different notes, of differing frequencies, the bridge's axis of vibration will constantly be displaced, not only transversally in the direction of the vibration of the strings, but also vertically, because as the frequency and intensity of the vibrations change so too there will be variation in the elastic response of the bridge and the belly beneath it.

To conclude: *The position of the bridge's axis of vibration will constantly vary within a given area.* This position can only be established for a particular frequency and a given degree of force exerted by the strings.

The science of mechanics tells us that a rotating mass can be maintained in equilibrium provided that its centre of rotation remains fixed. In a violin, on the other hand, everything vibrates around an axis which, however much one might like it to be immovable so that a simple and at the same time strictly scientific theory could be established, is unfortunately nothing of the sort.

These few indications of the obstacles barring the way to any solution of the problem clearly show what difficulties lie in wait for anyone wishing to establish a theory of the bridge such as could be regarded as fundamental to the system of mechanical and acoustical functioning of stringed instruments.

14

Mechanics of the Instrument, Bow Strokes, Output and Human Physiology

The strings of a violin are stretched between the tailpiece and the pegbox at a total tractive force of around 30 kilograms weight. If the strings were stretched parallel to the belly and very close to it, the instrument would behave like a beam bearing a disproportionate load on top and showing a tendency to bend. However, they are stretched through an angle at the bridge, thereby developing a force F perpendicular to the belly (Fig. 19).

This *component* force has the following *mean values* for the various instruments of the violin family, according to Bouasse[1] and other writers:

Instrument	Total tension in the strings in kg weight	Perpendicular force F exerted on the belly (Fig. 19) in kg weight
Violin	20–22 (also 30)	7–8 (also 12)
Viola	c.30	14
Cello	c.50	25
Double bass	c.170	108

Note: The values here given will vary according to the type of strings in use (gut or
     steel, etc.).

As Fig. 19 shows, the fingerboard must be fixed to the neck at a given angle to the belly so that the strings can be stretched at a given height above the fingerboard; then it will be possible to choose a bridge of the most suitable height so that the force exerted on the belly will permit the maximum fullness of sound.

The forces in play in a violin are remarkable when one considers that a fully assembled instrument weighs about 0.4 kg, and is a delicate and complicated mechanism. The tendency of the tractive force of the strings would be to implode the belly, to pull off the neck and to turn the fingerboard downwards, were it not for the fact that the belly is constructed in arched form in order to resist this

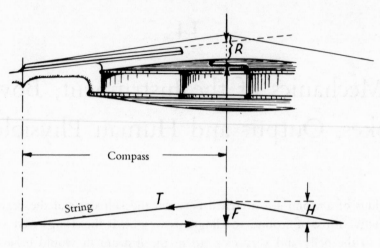

Fig. 19 Tension (traction) and pressure of strings
T: Tractive force of the string
F: Force exerted on the belly
H: Height of the bridge

force, reinforced along its length by the bass bar, and also to some extent relieved of pressure by the back, which gives support via the sound-post.

Every performer knows from experience the consequences of these considerable forces to which his instrument is subjected and which it must constantly withstand. If the strings are loosened the violin becomes more elongated, and when the strings are once again stretched the instrument will need a certain amount of time before it can adjust back to its original condition and produce its former tonal range.

We have observed the effect of the static forces to which stringed instruments are subject—forces, that is to say, which remain constant in time. But if strings are set in vibration by the bow, then further positive and negative forces, varying from moment to moment, are exerted on the belly in addition to the static forces already present.

The belly offers a different elastic resistance to each of the bridge's feet, since the right foot is situated near the place where the sound-post is wedged whilst the left one rests over the bass bar, thus in an area where it can vibrate much more freely. It is in fact to this ingenious asymmetry that stringed instruments owe their marvellous sonority.

The average weight of a violin bridge is two grams, and the minimum weight of a mute is around three grams; from this ratio it is possible to deduce what effect the alteration of the bridge's mass and moment of inertia will have on fullness of tone. (The *moment of inertia* is defined as the sum of the products of each individual element of the mass of the bridge multiplied by the square of their distances from the axis of vibration.)

If the bridge, sound-post and bass bar are regarded as a single composite element, the science of mechanics will enable us to explain something already regarded as axiomatic in the eighteenth century: at an equal pressure, the bow produces a sound of far greater intensity on the violin when it is drawn than when it is pushed across the strings.

The *Encyclopédie* of Diderot quotes a text of Jean Rousseau dating from 1687, as follows (for 'viola', read 'bass viol' or 'cello'):

... it is of great importance to use the bow methodically; and, as further proof of this necessity, composers mark the bow strokes in their pieces with precision. Moreover, we know that this is one of the distinguishing factors between the viola and the violin: the bow stroke is entirely the opposite for each instrument, so that what is drawn on the violin must be pushed on the viola, and what is pushed on the violin must be drawn on the viola. The reason for this is that in playing the viola the greater force of the arm is given to pushing and on the violin to drawing, because of the different manners of holding the two instruments; and it is for the same reason that on the viola long notes are pushed, short ones drawn—this not being the practice on the violin.

The theoretical investigations of Bouasse provide another explanation of why the sound of a drawn note on the violin has far greater intensity than a drawn note on the cello, whereas on the latter instrument the note will be louder if the bow is pushed. If the string frees itself from the bow at a given moment, it travels back in the opposite direction at a speed greater than that of the bow itself. If the bow is drawn, then on its release the string develops its highest speed from right to left, and its force passes to the belly through the left foot of the bridge, giving a much stronger percussive action and hence also a greater intensity of sound. On the cello the process is reversed. Why? The arrangement of the bass bar and the sound-post, in relation to the bridge, is identical. But relative to the violin, the cello is played turned at an angle of 180°. So it is easy to see why, this being the case, notes played with a pushed bow are stronger than those played with a drawn bow, and vice versa.

Many performers find there is no difference in intensity between notes played with a pushed or a drawn bow. Others admit that the difference exists, but, like Jean Rousseau, assert that the decisive difference lies in the power that can be exerted on the strings of a violin by the bow.

The first opinion was also voiced by Bouasse. He thought that this 'identical strength of tone' should be attributed to the correcting action performers make— often without realizing—by, for instance, exerting greater pressure on the violin when the bow is pushed than when it is drawn. Practical experiments reinforced his theory, which was also confirmed by neutral observers. One of his colleagues, a professor of physics who was also a good cellist, confirmed this as well: he repeated the experiments using a bow that was pushed and drawn at equal pressures and speeds.

We will allow the responsibility for Bouasse's theory to rest with the shrewd physicist himself, contenting ourselves with this mere summary in the hope that it will stimulate the interest of performers.

Though it is not easy to make perfect instruments, it is far more difficult to train outstanding players. Nowadays it ought to be felt an obligation towards music students that they should receive the most thorough examination at the outset of such an arduous course of study. It should be considered absolutely necessary to establish a procedure of selection in which the pupil's physiological aptitudes are tested too, as musical talent on its own is not sufficient for a long course of study of an instrument. The tragic situation has often occurred, for example, in which after many years a professional violinist has discovered all too late that he can no longer work on account of a persistent inflammation of the hand and the arm, because the physical exertion required appears to place too great a strain on them. It is equally devastating when a performer realizes that he lacks the necessary technique ever to attain the goals he has dreamt of.

Even the best teachers were until recently of the opinion that physical aptitude, if not exactly of secondary importance, was at least capable of being rectified, and was of little significance compared to talent and intelligence. At most, the size of the hands, the flexibility of the fingers and the mobility of the wrists were tested. Such empirical and summary tests cannot be judged entirely valid; for instance, in international competitions we often have the opportunity to admire brilliant Asian performers who possess relatively small hands. The really decisive factor is the total mobility of the limbs and above all of the forearm and the fingers; these are all physiological features that cannot be improved by even the most careful and assiduous exercises.

On the basis of brief personal experience, the present writer has always held that more attention should be paid to physiological aptitudes in the training of musicians. It seems astonishing that colleges of music by and large stick so faithfully to the narrow bounds of their traditions, and still devote so little attention to this matter, whereas in sport, by contrast, the physiological characteristics of athletes have long been taken into consideration. Yet in order to achieve a modicum of success, a soloist, in addition to his artistic talents, also frequently needs to be able to perform extraordinary feats of a physiological order.

In fact, anyone playing difficult music on an instrument as demanding as a stringed instrument will need arms, hands and fingers of uncommon strength and mobility. The performer must often remain extended to his limits for long periods at a time, and for such exertion he needs a quite exceptional ability to flex and stretch his limbs. The muscles will be contracted to an abnormal degree, and the small blood vessels which feed them thoroughly compressed. Circulation will consequently become inadequate, particularly when the muscles repeatedly undergo extreme contraction. Such excessive demands may go well beyond the physical powers of the performer, and he may begin to experience fatigue. This process is shown in Fig. 20.

If fatigue increases (positions 1–4 in Fig. 20), the effect of stimulus will become weaker and the ability of muscles to extend will gradually diminish. Likewise, relaxation will occur more slowly so that the supply of blood to the hard-pressed muscles is impeded and becomes inadequate. In the long run all this leads to a state of imbalance resulting in errors of performance; dynamic movements are no longer precise, and consequently rhythm and intonation leave something to be desired.

Professor Dr Christoph Wagner of the Hanover State Academy of Music and

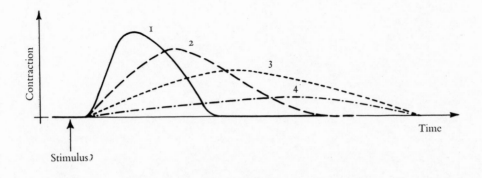

Fig. 20   Stimuli and contractions (after E. Grandjean)

Theatre, who completed a course in music after his medical training, has for many years concerned himself with problems regarding the physiological requirements for playing musical instruments.[2] His twofold training and experience led to the notion of establishing scientific principles for musical training, and developing special methods whereby the physiological requirements for playing keyboard and stringed instruments could be objectively established. These methods are currently being tested and applied at the Hanover Academy of Music. The aim of these investigations is to be able to recognize as such the factors which define the limits of technical performing ability inasfar as those factors are of an anatomical or biomechanical nature, so that due consideration can correspondingly be given to them in musical training.

15

Adjustment, Restoration and Sonority

The *adjustment* of an old instrument is a particularly tricky operation. The aim is to achieve the most agreeable fullness of tone, the finest timbre and an ideally even sound between the strings. Correct adjustment should also eliminate any scratchiness, shrillness, squeakiness and other defects of tone production. Only a very experienced violin-maker can make a really perfect job of adjusting an instrument.

The best bridge height—ensuring optimal static pressure on the instrument— can be found only by tirelessly trying out bridges of varying heights. It is equally important to check the angle and torsion of the fingerboard and to be able to correct this to give the most suitable elevation to the strings. Furthermore, it is necessary to establish—again by patient experimentation—what *gauge* and *type of string* will be the best suited to a particular instrument from the point of view of elasticity and weight.

If the sound-post is too firmly wedged it will give a stifled tone; on the other hand, it will lack power and sinew if it is too loose. It must be well matched both to the belly and to the back. It is of extreme importance to find the correct position for it. If it is too close to the axis of the right foot of the bridge, it will favour the higher notes, making them sound prominent, at the expense of overall tone production, which will then become more difficult. If the sound-post is placed too far from the foot of the bridge, the high notes will become weak and lacking in timbre. If the sound-post is placed too far over towards the bass bar, the low notes will suffer, and vice versa. Naturally the ideal position will also depend on the mechanical properties and thickness of the belly. The problem of the sound-post can be solved only by experimentation, and it lies entirely within the preserve of the violin-maker, though ideally he will have a performer to assist him in his tests.

Once the sound-post is found to be satisfactorily positioned, further experiments should be resisted (the compulsion to adjust being felt by certain performers immediately before a concert). Generally the outcome of such manipulations is merely negative, spoiling the correct positioning that has already been found and risking damage to the belly and the sound-holes. It is much better to aim at a better sound by trying out different types and gauges of strings. I recall the example of a performer, still alive today, who was the son of a violin-maker. He is very capable of adjusting the sound-post on his own violin, but is sensible enough to perform this delicate operation only once a year.

If the sound-post has been correctly positioned, the instrument will not necessarily require any period of adaptation for the sound-post and the bridge to settle down.

Only if it has not been precisely matched and fitted will a new bridge need a certain amount of time to adapt itself properly, as the feet must fit perfectly onto the upper surface of the belly. Periodically the angle between the bridge and the belly must be corrected as the strings, because of their tension, will tend to pull the head of the bridge towards the fingerboard. A 'list' of this sort makes an instrument easier to play, but also brings about a deterioration in timbre. If the bridge leans towards the tailpiece, a better timbre can be obtained, but tone production becomes harder. In this position it can happen that the violin will give out unpleasant notes that sound like wailing.

There are some notes, as for example the 'wolf note', which cannot always be eliminated either by precise positioning or by replacing the bass bar, the sound-post and the bridge. (The 'wolf note' is the husky note that can appear when certain notes are being stopped on the third and fourth strings of a violin. It is produced by a clash of vibrations and waves which are either out of phase or in phase opposition so that when superposed they partly cancel each other out.)

But these notes can also arise from other causes. We have seen that all the parts of an instrument vibrate when it is played. Therefore it only needs one of these parts to be out of true for it to vibrate out of phase or in phase opposition to the other parts, thus bringing about delays and failures of compensation in the emission of the note. Thus, a tailpiece or an excessively heavy cello spike may be responsible, or at least partly responsible, for an unpleasant note.

In a violin that has been poorly assembled or carelessly adjusted, it is above all the notes of the middle register that are vulnerable. The frequencies of notes in the upper register are actually too high for any ill-matched or poorly distributed masses to vibrate out of phase. For the opposite reason, the same is true of low notes too. What makes the instrument resonate and gives it its full sonority is the vibrating mass of the strings, and in every case this must be calculated so as to be well matched to the instrument.

If the note B is played on the second string of a violin it will sound quite different from a B played on the third string. In the latter case the note results from a different, in fact much smaller vibrating mass compared to the use of the second string, since to produce it the third string has to be shortened considerably. The interplay of vibrations between the oscillating mass of the string—or of any part of it—and the other parts of the instrument, and especially the belly, will be different in each case. And if a discrepancy arises between the oscillation rhythm of the strings and that of the mass of the instrument's parts, the sound emitted will be displeasing to the ear. In no case should the vibrations of the strings exceed the belly's capacity for vibration. Many defects can be easily rectified, but others again, as, for instance, too thin a belly or too thick a back, require very careful treatment. Such operations are extremely risky where old instruments are concerned: usually they achieve little, and sometimes their consequences are disastrous. Patching (or 'doubling'), if at all extensive, will fundamentally alter the acoustic properties of the belly and the back. But still more dangerous is any attempt to thin down the belly or the back; the damage resulting from such an operation will be totally beyond repair.

During the last century some fine violins were seriously harmed if not totally destroyed by the recklessness of many makers. 'There is nothing worse than active ignorance' (Goethe). Attempts were made to 'rectify' instruments by Stradivari, Guarneri del Gesù and other great masters, and ended by ruining them—a fact one can never sufficiently deplore. It is horrifying to read the memoirs of Count Cozio di Salabue (*op. cit.*) and learn of the massacre of many of Guarneri del Gesù's violins by the method of thinning down their backs. In mitigation it could probably be said for such repairers that they knew nothing about problems of resonance and would have had no idea of the laws of acoustics. The old masters of Cremona were well acquainted with the general notions of mass, vibration, frequency and resonance, even if they lacked today's scientific rigour. But by the time of the 'repairers' of the last century who thought they could improve old instruments, such concepts had passed into oblivion.

However, such ravages had unfortunately been taking their toll of valuable instruments even earlier. Already Abbé Sibire, who rates as one of the great violin-makers, writing in 1806, recalls examples:[1]

For example the belly has given way at some point: it is doubled. This means that it is planed down, hollowed out, then covered with a piece, either glued on or pressed into place, intended to be indistinguishable from the original. Doubling often affects the part of the belly or of the back where the sound-post is to be found: sometimes the entire belly, its edging, its ribs may be doubled . . . As the market value of an antique depends on its format, the violin may be enlarged or reduced in size. To reduce it may be acceptable, but to enlarge it! I leave it to the reader to imagine what happens to a belly's elastic homogeneity when it is enlarged by two central strips of wood, the one running lengthwise, the other crosswise. It appears that renewing the bass bar is a common procedure involving no risks. Sometimes the bar is replaced; sometimes it is doubled. In order to alter the curvature of the arching, the belly and back have even been known to be remodelled by the use of pressure, after being thoroughly steeped.

Sibire concludes that it is infinitely more difficult to repair an old violin properly than to make a new one.

16

Copiers, Imitators and Inventors

Together with the success of the great violin-makers, the making of copies sprang up as an industry. It was carried on by assistants or craftsmen who worked side by side with the masters. Living at close quarters wtih them in Cremona (see Fig. 1) these copiers had acquired considerable artistry through long years of apprenticeship. Many were even distinguished makers in their own right before they took to making copies. In those days the years of apprenticeship were very arduous. One need only read the conditions of an apprentice's contract, laid down unilaterally by the master, for this to be apparent.

It cannot have been very difficult to obtain 'facsimile' labels. Moreover, these would have the inestimable advantage that the paper, the ink and the gum were those of the period in question and thus bore all the hallmarks of authenticity.

But was it only the second-rate violin-makers who made use of the names of the great masters, or did the practice of attaching misleading labels perhaps come a little later, when violin-makers or the first dealers were more preoccupied with commerce than with art?[1] With instruments by makers as famous as Bergonzi or Montagnana there was absolutely no pretext for altering the trade-mark. And yet several of their fine instruments, which are marvellously constructed and finished, carry the labels of Stradivari.

The Ruggeris too were excellent imitators, as were later makers, such as the Sicilian Panormo, who lived in London. He succeeded in using wood from old English billiard tables to make instruments which for many years passed as genuine 'Cremona' violins, including the ex-Stradivari 'Balfour'.

As the tradition gradually disappeared and the love of fine instruments waned, the work of copiers too became rarer and more difficult. No-one would today venture to offer a connoisseur a first-rate instrument he had made himself and try to pass it off as a classic instrument, even if it had been aged by all the methods and artifices now available. Correspondingly, connoisseurs have developed their critical sense to such a point that for them an antique instrument is almost as different from a new one as a real diamond from an imitation one. Naturally, this applies above all to established experts, provided that they have no commercial interest and their intentions are honest.

For all the perfection of classic instruments, numerous researchers and experimenters have in the course of time made attempts to improve the basic shape of the violin still further. They have invented their own models in differing and remarkable shapes. Nowadays these survive only in the instrument collections of museums.

Recollecting the wilder flights in the annals of violin-making, we may be reminded of the short-lived triumph of Savart (1791–1841)[2] with his trapezoid violin, which was built by Vuillaume.[3] His work was endorsed by an award from the Academy of Sciences in Paris (with no less a figure than Cherubini on the jury); the efforts of Bagatella[4] too won a prize from the Academy of Sciences in Padua in 1783. Their ideas are now no longer spoken of, though once thought so revolutionary. Who today can remember the numerous authors, most of them professors,[5] and their countless works purporting to reveal all the 'secrets of stringed instruments'? Their writings have become virtually meaningless and are now read only for their curiosity value.

Naturally, the Russians have not been laggards in this contest to find the 'secret' of the art of violin-making. From the metallurgist Chernov (1911) to Professor Andreyev (member of the Russian Academy of Sciences); from the engineer Alender (director of the State Musical Instrument Industry) to the acoustician Yankovsky—all have had their say. Yankovsky constructed a hand-made model which then went into mass production. Its success was 'phenomenal': when in 1959 a jury of experts tested a sample batch of 44 together with a 'control' model (a classic instrument), results were obtained which 'astounded the world', according to Anfilov.[6] The Russians could not believe it, and the trials were later repeated, this time with a Stradivari, formerly belonging to Prince Youssupov, and a Ruggeri concealed among the batch: once again, the same amazing result. And today? Who now speaks of these production-line miracles?

The present writer has attended a number of competitions for the Paganini Prize during recent years. Many excellent Russian violinists have participated, yet none came to the competition with a Yankovsky violin. On the contrary, these young performers preferred old Italian violins to any others.

From time to time there have been reports of the triumphs of various researchers and experimenters; every single one of them has sunk without trace.

Their names have been quickly forgotten, whilst those of Stradivari, Guarneri del Gesù and their disciples still shine brightly in the firmament. Never since has the perfection of their work been rivalled, either in beauty or in sonority.

Often a classic instrument will sound less good than many modern violins at close quarters, or from the performer's standpoint. It is only from the middle or the back of a concert hall that the range of its tone and the richness of its timbre can be convincingly appreciated. In addition, it is generally much easier to effect transitions from *piano* to *forte* on such an instrument.

17

Scientific Testing and Stylistic Assessment

It must be said at the outset that *scientific tests* alone, even in the aggregate, cannot suffice to identify the maker of an instrument. They would be capable of *disproving authenticity or a particular attribution* rather than of establishing it. Nevertheless, such tests must be accorded importance as effective *complementary aids to critical and stylistic assessment.*

The merit for having extended methods of scientific research in the field of violin-making must chiefly to go Dr Max Frei-Sulzer of the forensic science department of the Zurich Police (Criminal Branch).[1]

Scientific tests yield chiefly negative results where an instrument is not entirely genuine or authentic. Such tests must be made before an examination on stylistic grounds is carried out. The experts who carry out the tests are required to possess a sound knowledge of physics, chemistry and spectrography. In stylistic assessment it is usual for other experts to be called upon, who will proceed from differing points of view.

Scientific tests naturally have their limitations. They must cause no damage, since an antique instrument is a work of art and must be preserved in its entirety. Its value lies above all in the beauty of its shape, the reputation of its maker, its state of preservation and its tonal qualities. In contrast to other works of art, it is also an object in use, and certain essential parts of it may have become worn or even misshapen over the years. Consequently, it has to be taken into account that in the course of time repairs are likely to have been undertaken in order to preserve the instrument and maintain the quality of its tone to the full.

In scientific tests it is only the original parts of the instrument that are investigated. Replaced parts, patches, or other elements that have been added subsequently by a repairer are not taken into consideration (except when faked, which indeed is often the case). Careful investigation can also establish repairs that are genuine, even where these are invisible to the naked eye.

Despite their limitations, the numerous scientific methods now at our disposal must be acknowledged as effective and rigorous. The testing of tiny splinters of varnish by *chemical methods* makes it possible to identify the general composition of the various layers of priming and varnish. It is thus possible to detect whether the composition of the first layers of original colour is typical of the supposed date of manufacture. Anachronisms may come to light, as when, for instance, the composition is found to contain colouring agents and resinous products unknown at that time. Study of 'microdots of fusion' or of softened tiny fragments can also help in ascertaining whether the varnish is original or not.

Optical testing is equally of great importance. *Ultraviolet light* having a wavelength of 3,130–4,000 Angström units is used, making it possible to compare coefficients of diffraction in order to confirm the results of chemical analyses.

Ultraviolet light from a *quartz lamp* (known as 'Wood's light') produces fluorescence spectra which will vary according to the composition of each varnish. The use of this lamp clearly shows up any retouching of poor quality; but there are violin-makers today who can retouch with ingredients that are difficult to distinguish from those of the original varnish even under a quartz lamp.

By comparing colour photographs of the various parts, it is possible to determine whether the scroll, the belly, the ribs and the back are coated with the same varnish or not. If on only one of these parts no trace of the original varnish can be found, we can deduce that this part cannot be authentic or, in the words used in certificates, that it 'does not belong'. It must be admitted that such tests are beset by pitfalls, and for this reason it is understandable, even though not justifiable, that certain violin-makers assert that ultraviolet light might damage the varnish. There is absolutely no scientific foundation for this view.

Almost no old violin in use today has escaped retouching. Investigation by fluorescence spectra reveals everything; but the results must be assessed by experts before correct and indisputable deductions can be made. Anyone unfamiliar with this practice would be horrified if he saw what happened to his beautiful violin under this light in the darkroom: it would look like a battered corpse floating in a cold stream by moonlight.

An experienced investigator who has a comprehensive stock of documentation on file can be of great help to stylistic judges in the authentication of an instrument by a particular maker by photographing the spectrum of the varnish and comparing it with that of an instrument of undoubted authenticity by the same maker.

A further kind of scientific testing is *investigation under a microscope*. This can reveal a great deal, whether it is conducted under normal or under ultraviolet light. Amongst other things it will reveal any artificial treatment of the wood by modern corrosives, showing up the presence of alkaline crystals. The microscope will also bring to light the difference between a fine transparent old varnish, which allows the formations of the wood to be seen in all their detail, and the varnish of a later maker or a copier, which will generally be virtually opaque.

Comparative microphotography makes it possible to compare the individual parts with certainty, as for instance the edges of the belly and the back, enabling the investigator to establish whether one of these parts was made with a different tool. In addition it can reveal whether the traces left by time and use on the exposed surfaces of an instrument are genuine or whether they have been produced by a forger using special tools, for example, to make tiny indentations which might appear genuine under normal examination. Microphotography can also be used to discover whether a varnish has been tampered with so as to appear old: tiny vein-like marks may have been brushed in here and there with the aim of imitating the typical cracks (*craquelage*) which occur in certain varnishes as they dry out.

There are also *methods of physical investigation* by means of which the approximate *age of the wood* can be determined. The most important and reliable of these is *analysing the relative concentration of isotopes*; this will establish the quantity of the radioactive isotope of carbon C14 contained in the wood, from which it is possible to calculate the date at which the wood was still part of a living tree. If, however, a forger uses wood of that date, taken from old furniture or ancient beams, the forgery cannot be detected by this method.

An old violin possesses a very characteristic sound spectrum which is quite different from that of a modern violin, as we shall presently see. Analysis of this too can be useful in certain cases.

Now we come to the tricky matter of *labels*. Old instruments which still have their original label are extremely rare nowadays, because unfortunately it has been the practice of previous centuries too to remove the label from a violin by a well-known maker and use it to give an aura of authenticity to another violin that may be partly a copy or a reconstruction. As we have seen, even at the time of Stradivari such subterfuges were perpetrated by contemporary violin-makers who are now comparatively well known, but who at that time were less highly regarded than the great master.

The authenticity of a label can be established by analysing the composition of the paper, though even that used by a forger may be from sheets or books of the period. More can be learnt, of course, by analysing the gum and the ink. It is also worth mentioning the possibilities offered by a comparison of a micro-photograph with a label of certified authenticity. As we have said, an original label may have been removed from one instrument and stuck onto another. Even in a case of this sort, scientific investigation can unmask the stratagem. Using Wood's light to detect traces of adhesive remaining on the wood, it is possible to discover whether the first label was of a different size, or whether the date inscribed on it has subsequently been altered.

It is often impossible to ascribe an instrument to a particular maker with any certainty without a *stylistic examination*, even though it may have been subjected in its entirety to all the scientific tests and proved to be both homogeneous in all its parts and of the required antiquity. For this reason, stylistic investigation is always necessary.

It is experienced violin-makers who make the most trustworthy experts. Family tradition and workshop experience have brought them into close contact with many fine instruments. They have taken notes, photographed and kept sketches and measurements of instruments and their various special features. These instruments have been sold, repaired, and often bought and sold again more than once. Violin-makers are therefore in a position to make comparisons and identify both a maker and a date. And to complement their experience in the workshop, further comparisons can now be made with the indisputably authenticated instruments of which very fine photographs are to be found in some excellent specialist books.[2] However, nothing can replace the flair and sure instinct of a violin-maker who has examined or restored hundreds of old instruments. Fortunately these experts tend to consult with each other, so that the last shadow of a doubt can be dispelled.

But even the best and most honest violin expert cannot be either technically infallible or exempt from human weakness, so that his judgement may unwittingly be influenced by various circumstances, such as for example commercial interest, either of a positive or a negative kind.

18

Acoustical Evaluation

We have already seen that in playing a stringed instrument, the performer will be producing mechanical energy by drawing the hairs of the bow across the string, and this will be transformed into another form of mechanical energy, that of vibrations. Only a small fraction of this energy is converted into heat, thanks to the instrument's high level of efficiency. These vibrations pass from the resonance chamber and the air contained in it to the outside air and thence to the listener's ear. This gives rise to a physiological sensation known as *sound*. Only part of this sound reaches the listener, depending on the particular qualities of the performer and of his instrument, the nature of the environment, and the listener's physiological sensitivity to sound.

The listener will not hear all the performer's variations of sonority, as these will depend on the quality of his instrument, the resonant or absorptive properties of the hall's acoustics, and of course the listener's distance from the platform. There are other contributory factors too, and we shall examine these in due course. It is clear, then, that the sound reaching the listener cannot be the same as that heard by the performing artist, but only a version of it that has been more or less attenuated by the factors just mentioned.

It is generally agreed that the performer himself is the best judge in matters concerning the acoustical quality of his instrument. But this is certainly not true; the player is at a diametrically opposite position from the listener in the acoustical environment. The sound directly perceived by the ear of the performer is very different from that which is experienced in the middle or at the back of a concert hall. As we have already seen, the original sound is a mixture of notes and harmonics. As it carries to any distance it becomes weaker, some of it being lost through absorption by the walls and through dispersion in other directions.

In classic violins there is a preponderance of fundamentals that are rich in har-

94

monics. These violins possess a pure sound of their own, often referred to as *voce italiana*—an 'Italian voice'. However, there are also violins, such as certain French violins of the last century and also modern violins of good quality, which, to the ear of the performer, produce a sound that is extraordinarily effective. But the amplitude of the harmonics of such violins is related to the amplitude of the fundamentals in a rather less compatible way; furthermore, harmonics and fundamentals in these violins get greatly absorbed and attenuated both in the air that is transmitting them and in the surrounding walls. These elements are of no benefit to the sound, and Germans call them *Schlacken*, meaning 'dross'. They do not assist an instrument's power or tonal quality.[1]

The performing artist may be utterly convinced that he can judge his instrument infallibly. Yet if we think of where he is judging it *from*, it is clear that his opinion can only be a subjective one. If he were in the position of a listener in a concert hall, and could take part in comparative tests, his verdict would be a very different one, in both an absolute and a relative sense. A well-known violin-maker tells how Landowska once made just such a mistake. From her position on the platform she found that the 'Vuillaume' that her partner was playing sounded much better than another instrument, which happened to be a little-known Stradivari. The violin-maker who was present suggested that she listen to the instrument from the hall. She was astonished at the result and immediately reversed her judgement.

The present writer has more than once witnessed the enthusiasm of distinguished performers for a modern instrument which sounded superb in the restricted space of a workshop. Great was their disappointment when they heard the same instrument in a large hall where numerous experiments were carried out with the help of a variety of players. Surprises of this kind are particularly unwelcome when a deal over an instrument has already been concluded.

From the point of view of physics, this circumstance can be explained by reference to the 'Residue Theory' of Shouten,[2] formulated in 1940. As we have seen in previous chapters, vibrations in the air caused by compression and expansion can be represented diagrammatically by a given number of sine-waves representing notes and harmonics. The frequencies of the latter will be multiples of their fundamental (corresponding, in mathematical terms, to a Fourier series). If only the fundamental is present in the vibrations and only its note is produced, this gives a pure tone which is determined solely by the frequency of the fundamental. When, in addition, harmonics are also present, a totally different aural sensation is produced: we hear a given note which differs from a pure tone in one particular respect—that of timbre or colour.

A person of particularly keen hearing who has sufficiently trained his ear can hear certain harmonics in addition to the note itself. In order to achieve this he must concentrate his finer perceptions on the various components of the note. This faculty our ears possess for analytically breaking down sound in accordance with the Fourier series has been known about for more than a century, having been pointed out in Ohm's Law of Acoustics.

We can demonstrate our ability to accomplish such an act of aural analysis with the help of a piano. The key of a note corresponding to a harmonic of a given fundamental is first soundlessly depressed. Then the key of the fundamental itself is struck, and immediately released. The note corresponding to the harmonic can then be heard, since the string producing it is free to vibrate in resonance.

Our sense of hearing does not generally avail itself of this ability, usually perceiving rather only a single note of a particular timbre.

Shouten made remarkable advances in experimental procedure and in the evaluation of sound spectra. He established that on the violin the fundamentals of some notes are very weak, even though perfectly easy to hear. This curious phenomenon becomes even more pronounced on the telephone. It has been found that even if the speaker does not raise the intensity of his voice, it can be heard equally well even when all frequencies under 300 Hz have been filtered out, although this is precisely the frequency band in which the fundamentals of male and many female voices are to be found.

Thus our ears can perceive a note that is in accord with the fundamental even though the latter may be largely or entirely absent. In his laboratory experiments, Shouten showed that listening to a whole set of harmonics can give the same sensation as that produced by a pure fundamental. These components he called the 'residue', and in physics his theory is known as 'Shouten's Residue Theory'.

This theory enables us to explain why a modern violin prominently endowed with harmonics can sound inferior to a classic instrument in a large concert hall. In the auditorium the degree of sound absorption depends on the walls, the hangings, the seats, the floor-coverings and the audience present. The higher the frequencies emitted by an instrument, the more these factors will tend to absorb the sound.

Two fine violins, one of them modern and the other an old one, each of the highest quality and possessing approximately the same strength of sonority, will yield differing sound spectra: the older violin will be rich in harmonics, above all in the lower frequencies, whereas the modern instrument will possess a super-

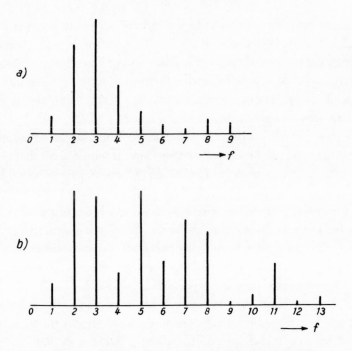

Fig. 21   Spectra of harmonics in male voice and violin

a)   Spectrum of the harmonics of the vowel A sung by a male
      voice on the note G at a frequency of 290 Hz
b)   Spectrum of the note G as above (290 Hz) played on a violin

abundance of harmonics in the higher registers, and will sound weak where the
other excels. A modern violin, moreover, which seems to the performer to have
a good tone, will on the contrary sound shrill (what the French call *criard,* and the
Italians *stridulo*) if heard from the auditorium.

A performer is in a better position to judge his instrument's *ease of emission* (in
other words, its promptness to respond and resonate) than its sonority. We say
'in a better position to judge' because such ease or promptness also depends on
the physiological characteristics and sensitivity of the performer. How often we
hear one player say that a violin is 'hard to play', when for another it 'seems to
play by itself'.

As we have seen, the performer cannot form a completely objective judgement
about his instrument, since he cannot escape the influence of the sound he is
accustomed to hear. His opinions can only become objective if other colleagues
play his instrument and compare it with their own, whilst he listens from the

back of a concert hall. From this standpoint he will be able to assess not only the sonority and the carrying-power, but also the balance of tone between the different strings and the timbre, both of his own and of his colleagues' instruments.

Timbre (see Chapter 6) is in fact a further factor that must be taken into account when evaluating the quality of an instrument. In a concert instrument this is the most important factor in producing *beauty of sound*.

The distance at which a note remains audible both in the open and in an anechoic chamber is referred to as the *carrying range*. It would seem that measuring this provides *the only non-subjective element* on which an *assessment of fullness of sonority* (though not of its *quality*) can be based. All other factors are dependent on the taste of the critic, and also on circumstances which are not always borne in mind at competitions, as for instance the condition of the instrument at the time of testing. A violin can suddenly lose something of its sound quality if it has been poorly adjusted, has been kept for a long time in a humid environment, or is being played by a heavily perspiring performer who breathes directly onto the belly (what a blessing a handkerchief can be!). Moreover, an instruments' potential performance can be affected by conditions in the auditorium; the tone of certain low notes, which can sound splendidly full in a half-empty hall, can become weaker as soon as all the seats are occupied. The mood and disposition of the performer can likewise influence the quality of the instrument being tested. The performer may be more or less unwittingly influenced by his sympathy for one or other violin-maker. (For instance, many swear by Stradivari, whilst others prefer Guarneri del Gesù.) He will also be aware whether an instrument is more, or less, responsive. If in a competition a change of player takes place it is necessary to take into account the variations of sonority and technique which will occur between one performer and another, as well as their different ways of bowing. It might almost be thought that it was the sonority of the performers and not that of the instruments that was being judged. If in such a competition, assessment rests with the public rather than with a jury of experts seated in a particular area of the hall, then a decisive factor will be the various positions of individuals relative to the platform. And finally, think of all the different shades of description that can be applied to the sound of an instrument; here, arranged in alphabetical order, are some of the terms the present author has met with: balanced, banal, biting, bodiless, brilliant, broad, colourful, discontinuous, distinguished, enchanting, energetic, flowing, fresh, full-bodied, grave, harsh, hoarse, hollow, homogeneous, meagre, mellow, melting, metallic, noble, pasty, penetrating, poor, powerful, pure, raw, rich, silvery, soft, superficial, thin, transparent, velvety, vigorous, virile, vivid, warm . . . and so forth. What, then, can be the criteria for an unclouded judgement of an instrument's tone, apart from its measurable carrying range? Yet the critic has to opt for a clear, precise and consistent verdict.

It is recorded[3] that at a cello competition in 1910, where every detail had been carefully prepared, the jury-member Marix Loevensohn said: 'No matter which instrument I was listening to, whether it was the Stradivari or the winning instrument, it was always the sound of Casals that I heard: despite the differences in timbre and in volume, the personality of the sound remained the same.' How many other judges, in similar circumstances, could make such a fine distinction as Loevensohn's between the part played by the performer and the contribution to be ascribed to the instrument's own quality and resonance? And how many performing artists could get as much out of a cello as could a Casals at the peak of his career?

We must ask ourselves how it comes about that modern instruments which have been listed as 'superior' after trials of their tone quality, and are the work of the finest contemporary makers, have totally passed into oblivion after only a few years. As we have seen, the evaluation of an instrument's sound quality is beset with uncertainty. Methods of comparison cannot be completely objective, since it is always personal opinion that decides. The sole factor that is quantifiable by using simple methods of measuring is, as we have already stressed, the sound's carrying range, in other words its intensity when heard from a distance in a hall. This intensity cannot be usefully measured on the basis of its quantity in physical and acoustical terms, but rather on that of the psycho-physiological nervous response perceived by the ear. This nervous response depends on the incoming intensity but is not in direct proportion to this intensity. In fact the observed response varies with the logarithm of incoming intensity of the sound. For this reason a corresponding logarithmic scale has been devised as a so-called 'gauge of sensation', graduated in units known as 'decibels'. Physical methods of measuring acoustical sensations also exist. But for these, complex machinery entailing a considerable degree of technical knowledge is necessary. In order to evaluate the listener's nervous stimulation, it must be measured in terms of a psycho-physiological scale, and this is done by means of a phonometer.

Dr Rohlhoff of the Greifswald University Institute of Physics has gone a long way towards explaining,[4] for instance, why the sound quality of a Stradivari or a Guarneri del Gesù has remained, after so many years, the sought-after but still unattained ideal. These violins have an 'Italian voice', a 'choice tone that is full and sweet'; it is a matter of an indescribable characteristic which has not yet been absolutely determined by means of concrete data. However, extensive investigations and experiments have enabled physicists to draw up in diagrammatic form typical characteristics of instruments possessing this 'Italian voice', and these show clear divergences from those of modern instruments.

Classic instruments have a voice of unusually great carrying range and an enchanting timbre. But apart from their carrying range, all essential characteristics, such as timbre, have until recently been impossible to determine by means of scientific measurement. Today, with the help of electronic apparatus, it is possible to draw up and compare diagrams representing old and modern violins: the frequency curves of harmonics and various statistical graphs allow us to conduct objective analyses of the tone and the timbre of an instrument.

The average spectrum of old violins is shown in Fig. 22, which shows the approximate relation between fundamentals and harmonics up to the thirteenth to be found on these instruments. As can be seen, there is a very pronounced fundamental with a wave-like falling-off of harmonics with crests occurring

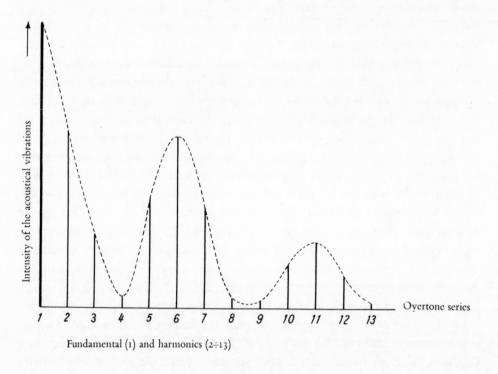

Fundamental (1) and harmonics (2÷13)

Fig. 22   Sound spectrum of classic Italian violins

around the sixth and the eleventh. Even in the best modern violins, a typical spectrum of this kind cannot be found. Its envelope curve bears a notable similarity to a damped sine curve.

These are the properties underlying the brilliance of tone and fullness of timbre which set classic Italian violins in a class apart from all others, whether modern, antique French, German or English.

Rohlhoff selected two types of violin—a Stradivari and a Guarneri del Gesù—from among the results of about 240 tests made by H. Meinel[5] and compared them with a first-rate modern violin. The Fourier analysis of sound vibrations measured in microbars and limited to the first ten harmonics of the note B (488.3 Hz) on the A string gave comparable results (see Fig. 23). A microbar is a millionth part of a bar, and unlike the usual psycho-physiological scale we have mentioned, it gives an absolute unit of sound pressure.

In the spectrum of classic violins we see a regular decrease in the strength of the vibrations after the first harmonic. This reaches a minimum at the fourth harmonic (about 1,950 Hz). Then the curve rises up to the sixth harmonic (about 2,930 Hz) but then falls away once more.

The spectrum of the modern violin does not show any similarly pronounced maxima. This also explains the subjective difference experienced when the two instruments are heard. In point of fact, on the G and D strings, classic violins by virtue of their excellent fundamental and remarkable harmonics have a fullness

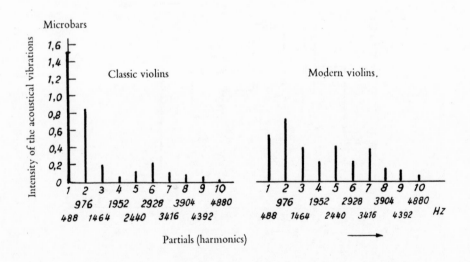

Fig. 23   Intensity of acoustical vibrations in classic and modern violins

of tone and splendour of timbre arising from the fundamental itself, whilst the harmonics of their higher notes are less pronounced. With modern violins the emphasis is reversed. In their spectrum the higher notes are prominent whereas the lower ones are soft and less highly coloured. This is particularly noticeable in double-stopping, where the higher note always dominates the lower one, a circumstance not met with on old violins, as with these the ear performs its own compensatory adjustments and perceives a balanced evenness between all four strings.

Meinel set out to use statistical researches as a basis for representing the properties of the best violins using diagrams (see Fig. 24) in which he showed the average frequency curves (mean acoustical intensity) for the various groups of violins he tested over each of nine frequency bands.

The first group consisted of three Stradivari violins (1715, 1717, 1719), one Guarneri del Gesù, one Santo Serafino and one Testore; all were in flawless condition. The second group consisted of six modern violins, three of which had been winners of German violin competitions during the year 1938. Finally, the third group comprised six German violins of average quality.

In the first frequency band the classic violins evinced a good intensity of sound with a good fundamental and a correspondingly beautiful timbre. In the second band the intensity began to increase until in the fourth it reached a maximum,

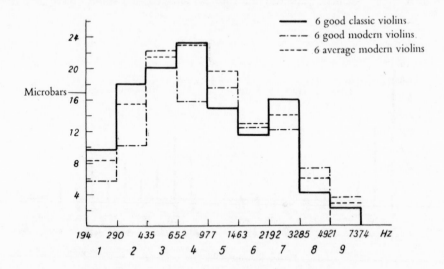

Fig. 24   Simplified frequency diagram for violins (mean values of acoustical intensity)

this being characteristic of all the best instruments. Fig. 24 shows how the irregular behaviour of the violins of average quality in the second and fourth bands is a disadvantage. The fact that they reach their greatest intensity in the third band gives them a sombre and spineless sonority. For all the instruments the fifth band represents a transition, whilst in the sixth there is a general drop in intensity, and in the seventh a further rise. Through the seventh, eighth and ninth bands we notice a beneficial falling-off, particularly in the older violins. This can be seen as a positive advantage, since otherwise the corresponding harmonics would yield sounds that were excessively piercing and harsh. In this respect too, old Italian violins show their superiority.

For every ten phons of increased sound intensity the human ear perceives a doubling of response. This means that between two harmonics in the spectrum shown in Fig. 25 a difference of ten phons will double the stronger harmonic in relation to the weaker one. (Unlike the bar and the microbar the phon is a unit of measurement on the usual psycho-physiological scale, and as a concept is comparable to the bel or decibel, though it is more useful from a physiological point of view.)[6]

In order the better to illustrate and confirm what has been said above, two of Meinel's (*op. cit.*) diagrams are reproduced below in such a way as to highlight

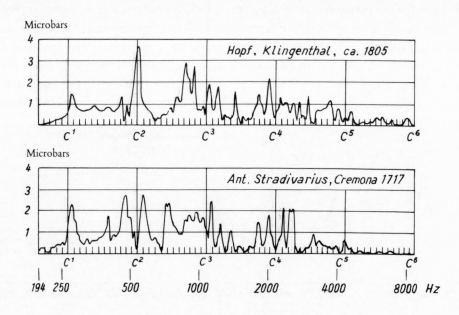

Fig. 25   Frequency response for two violins measured by H. Meinel

the difference in quality between a Stradivari dating from 1717 and a violin built by Hopf early in the nineteenth century (Fig. 25).

The diagram of the 1717 Stradivari can stand as a model for the ideal to be aimed for. If we compare the frequency diagram representing the sonority of the 1717 Stradivari with that of the violin dating from 1805, we see that the former has a peak resonance at around 400 Hz. This corresponds to the natural resonant frequency of the volume of air in the resonance chamber. The subsequent points on the diagram as far as the falling-off at around 650 Hz are the marks of an excellent violin, without the excesses of the other instrument, although that too is a fine one. Up to a frequency of just above 2,000 Hz the Stradivari possesses sufficient intensity of sound for the harmonics to produce a good response. In general, the spectrum of a good old violin will be characterized by strong response at the lower frequencies up to around 1,000 Hz, followed by a decrease with frequency up to 1,400 Hz then a further increase between 1,800 Hz and just above 2,000 Hz, with peaks at a lower level than those occurring in the lower frequencies.

This comparison of sound spectra between classic Cremonese violins and the best modern violins provides stringent scientific confirmation for what one already knows from countless subjective experiences, and it also establishes solid grounds for the preference shown by concert violinists for these instruments. For a wide variety of reasons the strength of sonority shown by modern violins on the A and E strings is for the most part wasted in the concert hall. The sonority of an old violin in the lower frequencies ensures that it possesses the sound and the marvellous timbre that is so characteristic of classic Italian instruments. The nature of its sonority on the higher notes will also ensure that these, too, have

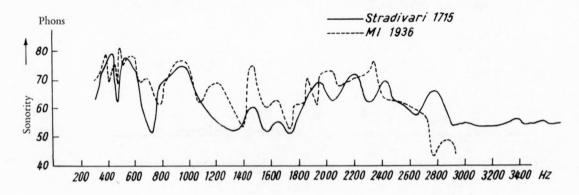

Fig. 26   Frequency response for two violins measured by E. Rohlhoff

good penetrative power without too much wastage of sound emitted in phase opposition and with a minimum of sound absorption on the part of the environment. And, for its part, the ear will reinforce its own perception of the higher notes.

Everything that has been said above can finally be confirmed by comparing the diagram of the D string of a 1715 Stradivari with that of the best modern violin Rohlhoff had at his disposal for his experiments (MI 1936). The intensity is given in phons for frequencies up to 3,400 Hz (see Fig. 26).

19

Electro-Acoustical Applications—
Electronics and Violin-making

A number of scholars, motivated by a love of music and an interest in electro-acoustics, have set about trying to discover a scientific basis on which to deal with the unanswered question: 'Why is the quality of classic violins no longer attainable?' In their work they have all been fortunate enough to have at their disposal instruments by the great masters such as Stradivari, Guarneri, Bergonzi and others, which they could compare with modern violins of the best tonal qualities and the finest craftmanship.

These researchers hoped that their labours might result in indications that would make it possible to construct instruments according to the guidelines of the great masters of Cremona. But the monographs in which they describe their experiments—mostly dealing with specialized areas—do no more than give a clear idea of the acoustical data yielded by classic violins, thus offering scientific proof of the excellence of many instruments. They are unable to say what to do in order to achieve the desired acoustical aims in modern instruments. This is hardly surprising, as we are here in the domain of art.

For decades, such investigators have been able to call upon virtually infallible and highly sensitive apparatus. But it is a tricky business not only operating such apparatus but also evaluating the findings it yields. The electrodynamic and electronic equipment designed for the detection and reproduction of sound is difficult even for a physicist to handle, unless he is a specialist in this field.

For the benefit of anyone wishing to pursue these matters in greater depth—and many of the findings of these investigations are of the greatest interest—there follows a concise survey of some of the most important investigations that have taken place in recent decades.[1]

As early as 1926, Bouasse,[2] in his university courses, predicted the sort of precision that the science of electro-acoustics would be able to contribute to the study of stringed instruments, particularly through the applied electronics that has since gradually been evolved from the premises of electro-acoustics.

The majority of researchers have made use of special aids such as an automatic 'bow' consisting of a ribbon permitting graduated variations in the pressure and speed of bowing, and special mechanisms to replace the use of the finger in altering the length of the string so as to produce different pitches; in addition they have used an almost inconceivably sensitive apparatus to control pitch, which adjusts instantly to give the exact note required in the same way as would a performer.

In order to obtain an objective means of judging timbre, most researchers have made use of harmonic analysis. This means they have separated out the fundamental and the harmonics so as to produce the diagrams or sound spectra discussed in previous chapters.

In 1920 Raman drew up diagrams of the harmonics of a fundamental in relation to the intensity of bow pressure exerted on an instrument. He proved that the timbre of a note played *piano* differs from that of the same note played *forte*. Saunders[3] continued work on the same lines as Raman, extending it to the measurement of sound production at different intensities; for this he used a microphone positioned at a given distance from the instrument. The 'efficiency' of a machine to transform energy—and this basically is what a violin is—can be defined as 'the ratio between the energy emitted as sound and the input of mechanical energy at different intensities and frequencies'.

The question arises whether the recording and measuring apparatus available at the time, with moving parts that could result in forces of inertia, may not have extensively falsified the results. It would be desirable at some time for a physicist to check these measurements of 'efficiency' using the perfected machinery now available: it is quite probable that we could expect surprising results were the 'efficiency' of stringed instruments as energy transformers to be investigated.

Meinel[4] went deeper into the matter, concluding that sound spectra can be affected not only by the manner of playing but also, and above all, by the physical properties of the resonance chamber, of the wood, of the instrument's shape, its thickness, and so on; in this way he made an estimate of the practical knowledge shown by violin-makers in their designs. Using condensers, Meinel sounded out the various parts of the belly and the back and was able to determine where their nodal points lay as well as establishing in which areas resonance occurred for each different note.

Meinel advanced our knowledge about varnish almost to the point it has reached today, and studied its influence on an instrument's sonority (augmentation of the mass and increase in the 'coefficient of elasticity'*). Unfortunately he did not succeed in deducing anything of practical consequence from his findings. It is

*See page 31.

possible that the instruments he tested did not possess the priming coat (ossification) we have mentioned as having been applied to the wood underneath the varnish proper. But in any case he must be given credit for having proved scientifically that the quality of an instrument's sound does not depend on its varnish to the extent that many people had previously asserted. For him the 'mystery' of the function of varnish was no more than an outmoded myth.

The discoveries of Rohlhoff[5] about the various speeds at which vibrations are propagated in wood are of extreme interest. With the particular methods of priming the wood used in those days (and this has nothing to do with the actual varnish used by Cremonese violin-makers) the speed of propagation found in classic Cremonese and other similar violins is quite different from that found in modern ones (see also chapter 10 on 'Varnish'). Some have attributed this to the age of the wood and to the fact that consequently it is of higher, though less regular, density than the wood of modern instruments.

Koch[6] came to a similar conclusion and put forward the hypothesis that in old violins the belly, back and ribs were soaked in a substance which 'homogenized' their wood. This narrowed the gap between the speed of propagation in the direction of the grain and that against the grain. According to Koch, the substance used for this and the method by which these eighteenth-century instruments were primed were both increasingly neglected until finally entirely forgotten.

Chambers[7] introduced a new method of setting the strings in vibration. He used a steel string (although this meant he was actually working with a denatured timbre), and when he wanted to produce a particular note, he set the string in vibration by passing variable-frequency currents through electro-magnetic coils.

The work of G. Pasqualini[8] was undertaken on behalf of the Italian National Research Council in Rome and proceeded on the basis of known methods. But from these Pasqualini created new procedures which served to eliminate most of the inaccuracies that had found their way into research findings as a result of the inertial forces latent in existing measuring equipment. Likewise, electronic amplification of vibrations was developed in the O.M. Corbino National Institute of Electro-Acoustics in Rome.

The results of Pasqualini's work can be summarized as follows. All violins possess good qualities of resonance at the low frequency of 60 Hz. Between 80 Hz and 2,000 Hz, good violins show favourable response and further maxima and minima; a poor violin will not have such pronounced maxima and minima in this frequency range, while it will display an excessive number of disturbing and spurious maxima in the higher frequencies.

20

Conclusion

It is not easy to define the best sound for a violin, since evaluation can only be subjective. We know that the great Italian masters made instruments whose sonority often differed notably from one to another. Even the sound of Stradivari's violins did not always remain the same. Throughout his long career he always had an eye to improving his violin designs. We can assume that only after some decades did he succeed in finding his ideal sonority. Today, too, violin-makers strive towards a personal ideal to which they devote all their powers. Even Stradivari's contemporaries changed the acoustical characteristics of their instruments in the course of time, probably so that they would correspond to the ideals of the age.

Naturally it would all depend on what the violin-maker considered the vital determining characteristic that went to make up a perfect instrument. Was it tonal power, readiness of response, brilliance, a special characteristic timbre, or some other factor? Each of the Cremonese violin-makers is likely to have more or less followed the taste of his times. Thus the Amatis made instruments that 'responded readily' and possessed a sweet tone, particularly on high notes. Stradivari and his pupils as well as Guarneri del Gesù earned the gratitude of posterity in particular for aspiring to and achieving an ideal of tone quality in which the marvellous sonority of the Amatis was wedded to the enhanced resonance and tonal fullness of their own instruments. In addition their violins also possessed greater carrying power, anticipating the acoustic needs of later ages.

It is indeed the lasting achievement of these masters that they seemed to look beyond their own times to answer the wishes and requirements of later concert performers. Today it seems incredible that at the time Stradivari was not considered the best of the Cremonese violin-makers. Bagatella records that in about 1780 it was Amatis that were thought of in the cultured circles of Northern Italy as the best instruments. In those days the violins of Guarneri del Gesù were even considered too brutal in their tonal power, almost 'aggressive' (Cozio Salabue, *op. cit.*). Stradivari was already more highly regarded since in his fine instruments he had succeeded in combining the sweetness of the former with the power of the latter. He achieved this perfection by respecting harmonious proportions between the individual parts and by his humanistically inspired love for his art. At no time did he ever create an unfinished work of art—he made nothing that was 'less than perfect', as Vasari wrote of Michelangelo.

For today's concert halls with their large dimensions, instruments of considerable fullness of sonority and carrying power are required; and Stradivari, Guarneri, Bergonzi and Guadagnini were making such instruments in the eighteenth century. It is extremely rare to find instruments made in other countries that have the same qualities—qualities that today's soloists find so satisfying.

At this point in our considerations we reach a very difficult question. Why is it that even physicists find these classic Italian instruments on the whole better than any others?

As we have seen, stringed instruments are resonators, and hence machines which convert mechanical energy into predominantly acoustical energy. The violin-maker's problem consists, then, in seeking out the *best acoustical solution* for the various parts of the instrument, analysing and matching them up so as to make of them a harmonious whole. After the celebrated great age of violin-making in the eighteenth century, violin-makers neglected the most important problems concerning resonance so that their art became degraded through simplification, indifference and ignorance.

It is no part of our intention to deny the beneficial influence either of mathematics and classical geometry (from Archimedes to Vignola) or of the Golden Section in the design and construction of stringed instruments. But if such factors could have been decisive in eliminating the uncertainties and puzzles that have persisted from the nineteenth century to this day, then Einstein, who gave some attention to the problems of violin-making, could have been expected to put something concrete about it into writing.

The problems of violin-making cannot be solved on the drawing board, but only through continual and assiduous experimentation and long hours at the workbench. By making mistakes and constantly trying again, the violin-maker learns to improve his technique between one instrument and the next. But it is not only the physical properties of individual parts that give stringed instruments their quality. The decisive factor, of course, is the sound of the finished instrument itself and the totally harmonious relation between all its parts once it has been assembled, varnished and given its final touches; and this is where the great violin-makers attained the summit of their art. Even the researches of Helmholtz and Bouasse did not go beyond such matters as the vibrations of the strings and of the resonators. Here the physicist must bow his head in wonderment. He has to recognize the limitations of science's contribution to the art of violin-making. The conclusion to be drawn from what we have said is that the scientist can do no more than provide certain guidelines for the analytical testing of individual components in the process of construction.

As a result of all the investigations that have been carried out since the beginning of the twentieth century, we know what is the ideal sort of tone and timbre for a violin. There is no longer much mystery about this, and yet it is still not possible to deduce unequivocal conclusions as to what particular features of construction distinguish classic Italian instruments from the majority of modern ones. Without trespassing on the domain of those admirable craftsmen who will always remain the best authorities on violin-making, we believe we can supply a few observations on the construction of stringed instruments that are worth pondering.

Unlike a sheet of glass or of metal, wood, an organic substance, does not possess a homogeneous texture. The speed at which vibrations are propagated in wood is greater along the grain and lesser against it (see Chapter 7). In an essay dating from 1923, Professor Koch stated that if it were possible to homogenize wood completely, one could obtain the same mechanical and elastic properties as are to be found in certain artificial homogeneous substances that are known as acoustically isotropic. He also declared that he had conducted microscopic examinations of classic Italian violins which revealed the presence of a substance that had penetrated the wood and homogenized it. He was on the right lines, but the conclusions he drew were not the correct ones.

There is a world of difference between this idea put forward by Koch,[1] so many years ago, and the results of the arduous and extremely precise investigations of Sacconi (*op. cit.*; and see chapter 10 on 'Varnish'). Koch sees the 'total' homogenization of the wood as the 'secret' of the great Italian violin-makers. Sacconi, on the other hand, considers that the benefit came from partial homogenization, an ossification of the wood, hence a process which 'corrected' the material but retained its original fibrous nature. If Professor Koch's suppositions were correct, total homogenization would bring with it a certain uniformity of sonority in all old violins, and the theories of Anfilov[2] could also be true, namely that instruments manufactured from compressed plastic or from homogeneous materials such as metals and so forth, would be just as good as the finest old violins, if not even better.

Anfilov predicted the following: 'The time is doubtless approaching when violins, cellos and guitars of the highest quality will be manufactured on production lines by automatic machines or simply pressed in moulds like cigarette cartons or soap boxes. When that happens, every violinist, whether he be a celebrated virtuoso, an orchestral player or simply a student at an academy, will be able to procure an instrument which, a hundred years ago, would have delighted Paganini. Is this a dream? Not at all. This possibility is entirely within the reach of the century we live in.'

Even on the basis of rational argument alone, it is easy to prove how ill-founded this assertion is. When the priming coat was applied to old violins, the speed with which vibrations were propagated in the wood[3] was altered, a little in the direction of the grain and more across the grain, because the pith absorbed more of the priming substance and on that account became less malleable. We may suppose that as a result of this priming of the wood the speed of propagation against the grain was doubled. A difference in speed of this order is largely sufficient to make a difference between the acoustic performance of a wooden violin and that of one constructed from a completely undifferentiated material such as, for instance, the one made of plastic which, as we have just seen, Anfilov thinks so highly of. The present writer is convinced that, because it is a fibrous substance, wood remains irreplaceable, since the quality of an instrument depends on the differentiation of speed with which the belly propagates vibrations.

Varnish alone has no such significant influence on sonority, though it helps by damping the vibrations of the wood. For practical purposes it leaves all the physical properties of the resonance chamber unchanged, owing to the compensation in the coefficient of elasticity.

On the other hand, the *priming coat*—sometimes mistakenly classed as varnish—is of fundamental importance to the quality of an instrument's resonance. It is also to the priming coat that we owe the marvellous effect of diffraction which, like a prismatic mirror, allows us to admire the pigmentation of the varnish proper in all its transparency.

As has already been mentioned, Sacconi stressed that Stradivari used a priming substance to bestow special properties on the wood, so that the master was able to use thinner bellies and backs. In spite of this partial hardening of the wood, its coefficient of elasticity was still significantly improved, as was the instrument's sonority. This 'treatment' has been forgotten with the passing of time.

If we observe the surviving moulds and models used by Stradivari, which have found their way back to Cremona after the dark ages of the last century, we can conclude that there are *essential differences in construction* between stringed instrument bodies built according to the old methods and those built by present-day methods. Internal moulds were used in assembling the chain of ribs so that it was easier to give them that slight, unobtrusive convex curvature which in many old violins cannot be measured but can only be felt by passing one's finger over it. This curvature caused the ribs to become more elastic—as they did not need to be so thick—and in this way the belly's freedom of vibration was also improved.

On the basis of these observations it is logical to conclude that there were no 'secrets' in Italian violin-making. These so-called 'secrets' consisted solely in a combination of factors and experience which today we may imagine but can hardly reproduce.

We must also take into consideration the fact that violin-makers of the twentieth century live and work in quite different conditions from those of their eighteenth-century predecessors in Cremona. The telephone, noise and ceaseless interruptions nowadays make it far more difficult to concentrate and to work with the sort of enthusiasm and inexhaustible patience necessary to raise this craft to the state of a noble art.

It must also be acknowledged that today's violin-makers live great distances apart from each other, whereas in Cremona they were able to live side by side (see Fig. 1) without ever being short of work and the means to live. That golden age could be compared with the Renaissance in Florence, with its abundance of talent represented by Leonardo, Raphael, Michelangelo, Botticelli and many others besides, all working in the same place and at the same time. Such miracles of simultaneous blossoming can also be found in Nature—we need only think of mushrooms, which will burst forth all at once, often in a circle, at the first sunshine after autumn rain. Similarly, men of talent can develop more readily, and often simultaneously, when cultural, economic or natural circumstances are favourable.

In Cremona at the end of the sixteenth century there were some very fine craftsmen in wood, who also specialized in inlay work. The work of Platina, which can still be seen in Cremona, remains exemplary even today.[4] From Brescia, where Gasparo di Salò and his pupils were active at the time when the Amatis were working in Cremona, the torch of violin-making passed over to Cremona, where it was easy to satisfy the ever-increasing demand for instruments. Today the vast demands of students, performers and orchestral players are largely met in the industrial centres of Markneukirchen, Mittenwald and Mirecourt, whilst today's specialist violin-makers are left with the tasks of maintaining early instruments and satisfying the needs of a few performers wishing to buy instruments which, whilst being of good quality, are not too expensive.

Under conditions such as these, how could the art of violin-making once again flourish as it did during the eighteenth century in Italy and elsewhere? And how many violin-makers would today have enough room in their workshops to accommodate whole tree trunks, or have at their disposal a granary in which varnish could be dried to perfection, as in Stradivari's *secador*?[5] Making an instrument is much easier if the wood is taken from the same tree trunk, and it is much more likely that a maker will achieve the sound he wants if he is familiar with the properties and peculiarities of his material.

In addition to these factors of historical environment, there is a further element: namely, the kind of personal knowledge and capability typical of all great craftsmen; this has dwindled and disappeared over the course of the centuries and cannot easily be handed down from one generation to another, being rather a matter of experience, technique and musical sensibility.

Yet in spite of everything, we perhaps need not lose hope that the art of violin-making might flourish once more. We should already have master violin-makers, were it not for the fact that everything today conspires against the art. Makers are individually scattered geographically, and this makes it difficult for them to exchange ideas or for there to be much possibility of passing on their knowledge to potential successors. The arduous labour of the father will discourage his sons from following on such a difficult path, which nowadays is not even particularly lucrative. Dealing in old instruments pays better, and violin-makers have to make a virtue of this necessity. Thus the best of them neglect their true calling, becoming basically merchants instead of artists. A hundred years ago, Vuillaume was one of the first violin-makers to venture part of the way along this path. And yet nowadays it would be far easier than in former days to pick up the essential groundwork in physics and acoustics; and the old methods of construction are no longer unknown. Yet time and incentive are lacking, since it is clear that such work will not bring the kind of financial rewards to attract young people. And there is indeed a job to be done in caring for and preserving the fine instruments of the past. Let us be idealistic in spite of the times and hold fast to the slender hope that the future will prove more favourable towards this art. Hasn't it always been such irrational ideas and hopes that have pointed to the future?

Meanwhile, performing artists are justified in preferring and seeking out classic Italian instruments. It is genuinely not just a matter of fashion: it is not the case—as many would believe—that an artist simply has to appear before the public with a violin by Stradivari, Guarneri or another great maker in order to make an impression. But today's vast concert halls not only require instruments possessing beauty of tone; they also demand fullness of sonority, and, particularly in this day and age, carrying power. Masters like Stradivari and Guarneri, as we have observed, seem to have had a prophetic foreknowledge of the requirements of modern concert halls.

If, for the reasons we have been considering, it is difficult to produce violins of such quality, what choice does today's virtuoso performer have? The present market value of a classic Italian instrument will often impose strict limits on what is available to him; one could pay a fortune for a violin which, when fully strung, would weigh just 0.4 kilograms, so that it is a sacred duty for anyone possessing such a masterpiece to allow some gifted performer the use of it.

Dante said that there are riches which make us the wealthier the more we bestow them on others.[6] He was thinking particularly of such treasures as civilization, art and science. In violin-making, Italy has given the world everything: experience, doctrine, designs and instruments. Very few of the instruments of the great masters have remained in Italy. Most are dispersed throughout the world, with the greatest concentration in wealthy and cultured countries.

Nowhere in the world is there a concert hall in which instruments by great makers like Stradivari, Guarneri, Bergonzi, Montagnana, Guadagnini and other famous contemporaries of theirs have not been played, bringing pleasure to all who have heard them. This is the splendour and glory of Italian violin-making, which spread outwards from Cremona through all Italy and bore fruit wherever it incited others to emulate it.

When the sound of a classic instrument rises above a large orchestra and reaches the back of a concert hall like a clear and luminous sword, a unique and exciting sensation seizes hold of the listener. The fame of the master who made that instrument, of which the performer is so proud, is constantly renewed at each concert throughout the world.

But how long can it go on? It is with some anxiety that I pose this question, since well-preserved and sonorous concert instruments are no longer very numerous: Stradivaris and Guarneris that have actually remained in use as concert instruments now number no more than a few hundred. For this reason, and from a deep conviction that what the Russian physicist Anfilov advocates is an absurd political theory, I believe that those who are still in possession of old instruments have the most profound obligation to preserve and look after them with care.

Instruments ought not to remain unused and behind glass; a violin that is not played on can be damaged by woodworm without showing any outwardly visible signs of it. The worms do not like either the varnish or the glue between the cracks. They bore long holes in the wood to avoid these substances before emerging, thus causing damage that is often irreparable. An instrument must be played with moderation and looked after 'with the attentiveness one would show to a woman one loves'. This was the opinion of the great violinist Ferenc de Vecsey. And it is true that a violin will not easily lose its qualities if it is played with care: only rough treatment and neglect, which is unfortunately what it gets at the hands of certain performers, will extinguish its life. An instrument will periodically need to be rested. Only if we treat these precious instruments with the greatest respect and care will our grandchildren—who are likely to be even more deeply immersed than ourselves in technological materialism—be able to enjoy such pure sounds as only they can give.

Like all the greatest virtuosos, Sarasate treated his violin, a splendid 1724 Stradivari, with extreme respect and tenderness. After his death, unfortunately, this violin was placed in a showcase in Pamplona and kept there. It is said that Ferenc de Vecsey was moved at the sight of it to exclaim, thinking of his own 'Maréchal Berthier' Stradivari: 'My violin must live on after me.' Unhappily, Paganini's Guarneri del Gesù suffered the same fate in Genoa as did the Stradivari in Pamplona: it only emerges into the light of day once a year at the Paganini Competition and very rarely otherwise.

After everything that has been said in this book, it should be apparent that violin-making is one of the most difficult of all the arts to pursue, because of the large measure of intuition it requires. The great Cremonese maker Giovanni Battista Guadagnini was a paragon of this intuitive art. He led a wandering existence, moving from Cremona to Piacenza and Milan, returning to his native town, and leaving again for Parma and later Turin, constantly seeking good fortune and success (but in spite of all, spending much of his life a poor man). This versatile and highly talented artist was virtually an illiterate, as his patron in Turin, Count Cozio di Salabue, was able to confirm. G. B. Guadagnini left us some excellent instruments, markedly different amongst themselves, since in his travels he was obliged to use woods and varnishes of extremely varied quality. Nonetheless, his instruments are all genuine masterpieces and possess an outstanding concert sonority.

The art of violin-making is not only one of the hardest of arts to practise, but it also has something of magic about it, since makers are working with materials that are still alive and using them to create instruments with the perpetual power of arousing live feelings.

It is sad indeed to record the fact that this art is slowly dying out, despite the heroic efforts of a few living violin-makers: the progress of mass civilization and ill-used technology is slowly but relentlessly extinguishing the last glimmers of that Renaissance humanism of which man in the twentieth century has so great a need.

Notes

Index

Notes

1: INTRODUCTION

1. S. F. Sacconi, *I 'Segreti' di Stradivari* (Illustrazione del procedimento costruttivo), Cremona, 1972.
2. O. Miggé, *Das Geheimnis der berühmten italienischen Geigenbauer*, Frankfurt a.M., 1895.
   C. Schulze, *Stradivaris Geheimnis*, Berlin, 1901.
   A. Jarosky, *The secret of the Italian Violin Makers*, London, 1935.
   M. Boger, *Das Geheimnis der Stradivari*, Berlin, 1944.
   Also many other authors.
3. F. J. Fétis, *Stradivarius et recherches sur l'origine et les transformations des instruments à archet*, Vuillaume, Paris, 1856.
4. R. Bacchetta, *Stradivari*, Soc. Ed. Cremona nuova, 1937 and 1967.
5. A. Puerari, *Le tarsìe del Platina*, Banca Popolare di Cremona, 1967.

2: THE VIOLIN-MAKER'S ART

1. S. Baglioni, *Elementi fisiologici della parola e della musica*, Rome, 1925.

4: ORIGINS OF THE VIOLIN'S SHAPE, AND SOME CURIOSITIES OF ITS HISTORY

1. Léonard de Vinci, . . . *l'expérience, le maître des maîtres*, Friedesthal-Hachette, 1965.
2. G. Anfilov, *Physique et Musique*, Ed. Mir, Moscow, 1969.
3. See R. Bacchetta, *op. cit.*
4. F. J. Fétis, *op. cit.*

6: STRINGS AND SOUNDS

1. H. Bouasse, *Acoustique—Cordes et membranes*, Delagrave, Paris, 1926.
2. H. Helmholtz, *Die Lehre von den Tonempfindungen*, 1862.

7: THE WOOD

1. W. H., A. F. and A. E. Hill, *Antonio Stradivari*, W. E. Hill & Sons, London, 1902.
2. F. Hamma, *Meisterwerke italienischer Geigenbaukunst*, Hamma, Stuttgart, 1931.
   W. Hamma, *Meister italienischer Geigenbaukunst*, Schuler, Stuttgart, 1964.
3. H. K. Goodkind, *Violin Iconography of Antonio Stradivari*, Larchmont, New York, 1972.
4. F. Savart, *Mémoire sur la construction des instruments à cordes et à archet*, Deterville, Paris, 1819.
5. Koch, Umschau, Vol. 24, 1923.
6. A. Bagatella, *Regole per la costruzione de' violini, viole, violoncelli e violoni*, Memoria presentata alla R. Accademia di Scienze Lettere ed Arti di Padova, 1786.

8: THE BODY: BELLY, SOUND-HOLES, RIBS AND BACK

1. Moeckel-Winckel, *Die Kunst des Geigenbaues*, Berlin, 1954.
2. A. Roussel, *Traité de lutherie*, Paris, 1966.
3. M. Sibire, *La chélonomie ou le parfait luthier*, Brussels, 1806.
4. F. J. Fétis, *op. cit.*

10: THE VARNISH

1. S. F. Sacconi, *op. cit.*
2. A. Puerari, *op. cit.*
3. A. Cozio di Salabue, *Carteggio*, Cordani, Milan, 1950.
4. Droegemeyer, *Die Geige*, Berlin, 1903.
5. H. Meinel, *Über Frequenzkurven von Geigen*, Akustische Zeitschrift, 1937.

12: HOW STRINGED INSTRUMENTS FUNCTION

1. H. Helmholtz, *op. cit.*

13: TOWARDS A THEORY OF THE BRIDGE

1. H. R. Haweis, *Old violins, and violin lore*, London, 1898.

14: MECHANICS OF THE INSTRUMENT, BOW STROKES, OUTPUT AND HUMAN PHYSIOLOGY

1. H. Bouasse, *op. cit.*
2. C. Wagner, *Physiologische Voraussetzungen für das Geigenspiel* (Int. Kongr. Graz, 1972); *Die Messung rheologischer Grössen an Gelenken der menschlichen Hand*, Wissensch. Konf. Deutscher Naturforscher und Ärzte (Springer Verlag, 1974); *Determination of Finger Flexibility*

(European Journal of Applied Physiology, 1974); *Der Instrumentalunterricht*, Musik und Bildung, 1975, Ed. Schoof.

15: ADJUSTMENT, RESTORATION AND SONORITY

1. M. Sibire, *op. cit.*

16: COPIERS, IMITATORS AND INVENTORS

1. A. Vidal, *Les instruments à archet*, Paris, 1786.
2. F. Savart, *op. cit.*
3. M. Sibire, *op. cit.*
4. A. Bagatella, *op. cit.*
5. K. Fuhr, *Das akustische Rätsel der Geige*, Leipzig, 1926.
6. G. Anfilov, *op. cit.*

17: SCIENTIFIC TESTING AND STYLISTIC ASSESSMENT

1. M. Frei-Sulzer, *Naturwissenschaftliche Methoden zur Aufdeckung von Geigenfälschungen*, Archiv für Kriminologie, Ed. 116, Vol. 5/6, Schmidt-Römhild, Lübeck, Nov.–Dec. 1955.
2. F. and W. Hamma, *op. cit.*
   W. H., A. F. and A. E. Hill, *op. cit.*
   E. N. Doring, *The Guadagnini Family*, Chicago, 1949.
   H. K. Goodkind, *op. cit.*

18: ACOUSTICAL EVALUATION

1. See also: Pasqualini-Briner, *Nota circa gli effetti dell'assorbimento ambientale del suono dei violini antichi e moderni*, Fratelli Bocca, Milan, 1950.
   D. Boyden, *The History of Violin Playing from its Origins to 1761 with Record of Comparative Examples Played by A. Loveday*, Oxford University Press, Oxford and London, 1965.
2. J. F. Shouten: *Die Tonhöhenempfindung*, Philips Technische Rundschau, 5te Jahrg., Vol. 10.
3. D. J. Chenançais, *Le violoniste et le violon*, Nantes, 1911.
4. E. Rohlhoff, *Der Klangcharakter altitalienischer Meistergeigen*, Zeitschrift für angewandte Physik, 4/1950.
5. H. Meinel, *Zur schalltechnischen Prüfung der klanglichen Qualität von Geigen*, Zeitschrift für technische Physik, 1938; Akustische Zeitschrift, 1939 and 1940.
6. E. Luebcke, *Naturwissenschaft*, 1938 (so-called 'meaning of acoustical intensity' after Fletscher and Munson).

19: ELECTRO-ACOUSTICAL APPLICATIONS—ELECTRONICS AND VIOLIN-MAKING

1. E.g. G. Pasqualini, *L'électroacoustique appliquée à la lutherie*, Rome, 1953.
2. H. Bouasse, *op. cit.*
3. F. A. Saunders, *The mechanical action of violins*, Journal of the Acoustical Society of America, 1937.
4. H. Meinel, *op. cit.*, 1937.
5. E. Rohlhoff, *op. cit.*
6. Koch, *Das Geheimnis der altitalienischen Meistergeigen*, Westermanns Monatshefte, June 1924.
7. F. Chambers, *Notes on the resonance of a violin*, Phil. Magazine, London, 1928.
8. G. Pasqualini, *op. cit.*; also *Elettroacustica applicata alla liuteria*, Annuario della R. Accademia di S. Cecilia, Rome, 1938/39; *Proprietà del corpo di risonanza degli strumenti ad arco rilevate con metodi elettroacustici*, Annuario della R. Accademia di S. Cecilia, Rome, 1938/39; *Nuovi risultati conseguiti nello studio della cassa armonica dei violini con metodi elettroacustici*, La ricerca scientifica, Rome, 1943.

20: CONCLUSION

1. Koch, *op. cit.*, 1923.
2. G. Anfilov, *op. cit.*
3. F. Savart, *Sciences mathématiques, physiques et naturelles*, L'Institut, Paris, 1818.
4. A. Puerari, *op. cit.*
5. A. Cozio di Salabue, *op. cit.*
6. Dante, *De Vulgari eloquentia*.

Index

Fourteen Classic Violins

from the collection of concert instruments
'Great Artists'

Photographs by A. Papafava dei Carraresi
and (Plates V and VI) Zonda

Egr. dott. Ing. Paolo Peterlongo
di Milano

Con particolare ammirazione
per la passione e perizia con
cui ha saputo riunire una
delle più belle collezioni d'Europa
di violini classici

Simone F. Sacconi

da Cremona
25 Novembre 1972

Dott. Ing. Paolo Peterlongo
of Milan:

In profound admiration for the inspiration and knowledge with
which you have assembled one of the finest European collections
of classic violins

Simone F. Sacconi
Cremona
25 November 1972

The Plates

I. NICOLO AMATI 'SCOURDILLE'

Cremona, 1651 (ex Vatelot)

The best known and most important violin-maker of the Amati family—founders of the Cremona school—was Nicolo, son of Hieronymus I (or Gerolamo), born in Cremona in 1596. De Piccolellis, in his treatise *Ancient and Modern Violin Makers* (1885), writes authoritatively of Nicolo and his school, and of the 'important changes' he introduced in the construction of stringed instruments.

In his mature period Nicolo Amati discovered a number of 'laws' which he went on to use consistently in the construction of his instruments. These led him along a different path from that followed by his father Gerolamo and his uncle Antonio, and from this time onwards his instruments differ considerably from theirs. They are perfect creations, distinguished by rare elegance and purity of form. They bear witness to the work of a true artist: every detail is thoroughly thought out. The above-mentioned innovations are the fruit in the first place of Nicolo's artistry and his acquired scientific knowledge, and secondly of his ever-growing experience (see von Lütgendorff),* through which he reached the highest pinnacle of the violin-maker's art as it was practised in his time. His faithful and conscientious pupils, such as Antonio Stradivari (who did not leave his workshop until 1667), Domenico Montagnana and Giovanni Battista Rogeri of Bologna, who later worked in Brescia, testify to Amati's achievement.

The violin shown here is one of the finest examples of Nicolo's art. It is 354 millimetres in length, thus one of the maker's larger models. The varnish, of a glorious golden orange colour, shows off the broad curl of the maple back and the beauty of the pine belly. This choice instrument is now more than three and a quarter centuries old, yet remains in an excellent state of preservation. Its timbre is sweet, and its warm tone—as in all the best preserved instruments of Amati—has such carrying power that it can be played to good effect by a soloist even in the large concert halls of today.

This 1651 Nicolo Amati soon found its way to France. It eventually came into the possession of Marcel Vatelot, who in 1951 sold it to Professor Maurice Scurdille. In 1968 it returned to Italy.

*For details of publications of authors mentioned on pages 132–58, see Bibliography to the Plates, page 160.

II. GIOV. BATTISTA ROGERI (ROGERIUS) 'MILANOLLO'

Brescia, 1701

G. B. Rogeri was born in Bologna in 1650, and went to Cremona to become apprenticed —at the same time as the young Antonio Stradivari—to Nicolo Amati, already a famous master. In about 1680 he started his own workshop in Brescia, working there until his death in 1730. He survived the terrible years of the plague, to which many of his violin-making colleagues fell victim, and subsequently played a decisive role in the revival of the art of violin-making.

Rogeri was one of the finest of all makers. His violins and cellos are still much in demand as concert instruments.

The 1701 violin shown here was played at many concerts by Igor Oistrakh whilst his own instrument was being overhauled in Paris. It is accounted 'one of the finest of the few surviving examples of this master's work' (Etienne Vatelot).

The instrument's back consists of a single piece of maple, with a broad curl descending to the right. The belly is of attractive pine, fine-grained at the centre, opening towards the flanks. The violin is 354.5 millimetres long and its shape is of rare elegance. The ribs too are of broad-curl maple. The scroll, although of rather plain maple, is wholly typical of this maker's brilliant work. The varnish is of a rich orange colour on a golden ground.

The instrument is in an excellent state of preservation. A coating of rosin around the bridge area proves how much it has been played.

III. ANT. STRADIVARIUS
'CONTE DE FONTANA'
Cremona, 1702 (ex D. Oistrakh)

According to tradition this violin used to belong to the violinist Ferrari, who at the time lived in Paris, having been a pupil of Tartini together with Nardini. Ferrari is said to have been the first violinist to have used *flautando*. Later the instrument returned to Italy and was recommended by the Milan violin-maker Bisiach to the Count of Fontana. The latter acquired it and kept it for many years at his villa in Belgirate on Lake Maggiore. On the death of the Count it went to a collector, Foltzer, and later, with the Parisian firm of Vatelot acting as intermediary, passed into the hands of David Oistrakh.

Oistrakh remained faithful to this violin throughout the period when he was at the height of his powers, in fact, until a few years before his death. During his last years he thought longingly of this first Stradivari that he owned, and played all over the world for a period of some decades.

The instrument has a fine broad tone and an enchanting timbre. Doubtless it is this violin that Oistrakh played on most of his gramophone recordings.

Like the 'Tuscan' and the 'Auer', this violin is a typical product of the great Cremonese master's middle period. It still bears its original label, dated 'Cremona 1702'. The belly is remarkable and a great rarity in that it consists of a single piece of beautiful pine. The wavy grain is fine at the centre and opens towards the flanks. The certificates from the firms of Hill and of Marcel and Etienne Vatelot lay particular stress on these details. Despite its age, the instrument is excellently preserved, and of unusually solid and powerful character.

Another especially delightful feature is the varnish, highly typical of its period, and preserved almost in its entirety. Its colour, according to the definition of the Verband der Schweizer-Geigenmacher, is 'of a classic gold-tinged orange-brown', and it is beautifully transparent. This varnish possesses a remarkable thermoplasticity, and under the magnifying glass displays a charming natural *craquelage*, a characteristic feature of many Cremonese instruments.

This instrument has been described by numerous authors, receiving special emphasis, with illustrations, in Sacconi (p. 193) and H. K. Goodkind (pp. 320–21).

IV. ANT. STRADIVARIUS
'MARÉCHAL BERTHIER'
Cremona, 1716 (ex Ferenc von Vecsey)

'An instrument of divine beauty, with a tone that is sweet yet powerful, and a deep timbre. How enchanting it is to play on.'
(David Oistrakh, Berlin, 1972)

Alexandre Berthier, Marshal of France and Prince of Neuchâtel, obtained this violin from Napoleon Bonaparte (probably as booty from the war in Spain).

Records of contemporary violin-makers suggest that the violin was later acquired by Vuillaume. In 1895 it passed into the hands of a French aristocratic family and thence to the violin-maker Germain in Paris. The Stuttgart firm of Hamma & Co. became the next owners in 1909. Hardly was the 'Berthier' in their possession when Caressa, a Paris violin-maker, sent Hamma a telegram asking him to bring the instrument to Geneva immediately as there was a prospective buyer. But in fact it was the Vecsey family in Berlin who were interested in it. Baron Vecsey de Vecse acquired it for his then sixteen-year-old son, who played it at all his concerts right up to his death in 1935.

As The Strad magazine reported (London, July 1911, vol. 22, no. 255), the 'Maréchal Berthier' Stradivari was marvellously preserved (as it remains to this day) and 'entirely free from cracks'. In the words of The Strad's description: 'The varnish with which it is still plentifully covered is the master's favourite orange-red; the tone is large, sonorous, and eminently suited for the concert-hall. The form is that said to have been adopted by Stradivari in about 1708–09, the widths being full, and the length of body $14\frac{1}{8}$ inches. The back is of the fine, broadly-marked maple seen in numbers of the maker's instruments of this, his best period. There appears to have been in one place a piece of faulty material, which Stradivari himself covered up with a small V-shaped veneer; but this is invisible, or nearly so in photographs.' (The master apparently wished to make use of the acoustical properties of this little 'soundboard' at the back of the instrument.)

Today too this violin is accounted an instrument of extraordinary beauty and exceptional fullness of tone. Such violinists as Principe, David Oistrakh, Szeryng, Francescatti, Grumiaux, Kogan, Gulli, Brengola and many others have expressed admiration for it. It is one of the few violins of the great master that are still in an excellent state of preservation and possess the powerful and warm tone demanded by today's large orchestras and concert halls.

The instrument is described in many books, notably in Henley, Doring and Fritz Meyer. It is also illustrated in the Fridolin Hamma and Walter Hamma books, S. F. Sacconi (p. 173), and H. K. Goodkind (pp. 478–9).

V. PETRUS GUARNERIUS II
'FRANCISCO COSTA'
Venice, 1735 (ex Vidoudez)

In the same year that Giuseppe Guarneri, called 'del Gesù', built the Barons Knoop-Gutman instrument (see Plate VI), his younger brother Pietro II produced this violin in Venice. He had settled there after working with his brother in the Cremona workshop of their father and later in that of his uncle Pietro in Mantua. After a lifetime devoted to his work, he died in Venice in 1762.

Pietro Guarneri was thoroughly individual and independent in the practice of his art, though we may sometimes find the influence of his uncle Pietro of Mantua and of the great Cremonese Venetians, such as Sanctus Seraphin and Montagnana, when we look at his magnificent varnishes. He would sometimes use the splendid red varnish to be found in his 1743 violin illustrated in Plate X; at other times, the varnish has a golden-orange hue as in the present instrument, and is comparable to that of the Sanctus Seraphin shown in Plate IX.

This 1735 violin is an extraordinary instrument, not simply on account of its shape and the graceful line of its sound-holes, its fine scroll and the marvellous transparency of its varnish, but also because of its tone and great carrying power, as well as its timbre, which is characteristic of this great master. It has been described as 'absolutely first-class'; 'it speaks and plays almost by itself with its particularly lovely tone' (Ruxandra Colan).

In 1916 the instrument was acquired by the famous Spanish violinist Francisco Costa—after he had long been searching for a concert violin—from the London firm of Hill, and he played it up to his death.

The back is made from two pieces of maple with irregular wavy grain in the middle. The belly has moderately broad grain narrowing towards the flanks. The very fine scroll, which has plainish curl, and the ribs are also of maple. The instrument has been preserved to perfection and represents a typical specimen from the Cremonese master who was able to find in Venice woods in no way inferior to those obtainable in Cremona. His violins are very much sought after, since they are excellent and characteristic 'concert instruments'.

This violin is accompanied by certificates from the firm of Hill in London and from Pierre Vidoudez in Geneva.

VI. JOSEPH GUARNERIUS 'DEL GESU'
'BARONS KNOOP/GUTMAN'
Cremona, 1735

Giuseppe Guarneri was a son of Giuseppe Giovanni Battista (also known as 'filius Andrea') and a brother of Pietro, the 'Cremonese from Venice', also known as Petrus II. He is the best known of all the members of the famous Guarneri family. The nickname 'del Gesù' was given him on account of the imprint on his labels. In his earlier years he worked together with his brother in his father's workshop, but soon set up independently and produced masterpieces whose individuality and fullness of tone were to arouse the admiration of a later age. In his own time he was not accorded the respect he deserved, so that in the time of Count Cozio di Salabue his violins could be bought at utterly disproportionate prices.

Guarneri del Gesù created his own model which he constantly improved and which attained classic status. He pursued his own ideas without imitating his contemporary Antonio Stradivari either in the shape of the body, the cut of the sound-holes, or the curvature and thickness of the belly and back. He appears rather to have taken his inspiration from the last products of Gasparo da Salò, which suggested new possibilities to him (see George Hart).

His output was not large. Messrs Hill assert that he built no more than two or three hundred violins. According to other writers, the number was even lower. His instruments are therefore especially rare; on account of their sonority and timbre, those of the 'second' and 'third' periods (see Antoine Vidal) produced after 1730 are highly treasured.

As with nearly all violins of this category the 1735 del Gesù illustrated here bears the names of its former owners: Baron Knoop of London and subsequently Baron Gutman. Both were well known as collectors who possessed considerable knowledge of violins. This violin is depicted in W. Hamma and is mentioned by Vannes and others. It possesses a very beautiful, strong scroll in del Gesù's characteristic form, and a back made from two pieces of maple with small horizontal wavy curl. The pine belly has narrow grain, broadening towards the edges. The colour of the remarkably beautiful varnish is golden orange. The sonority and timbre of this violin as heard in a large hall such as that of La Scala have been highly praised by connoisseurs: 'Its sound is human; the violin is sensitive and easy to play' (Mariana Sirbu).

The instrument is accompanied by a certificate from the firm of Herman, New York, dating from 1931 when the firm was managed by Sacconi; there is also a certificate from Pierre Vidoudez of Geneva.

A Central European collector wanted this violin to be included, even if only temporarily, in the collection 'Great Artists' so as to give a more complete survey of the work of the great Cremonese makers.

VII. DOMENICO MONTAGNANA 'MARSICK'
Venice, 1738 (ex Möller)

It is remarkable how little we know about this great master, who was one of the finest violin-makers of classical times; it is also strange how rare his instruments are—at least the authentic ones. It is not known for certain in whose workshop 'the mighty Venetian', as C. Reade calls him, served his apprenticeship. However, he was probably an apprentice in Cremona with Nicolo Amati, at the same time as Stradivari, and subsequently, on the master's death, he may well have followed his colleague and friend Antonio when the latter set up his own workshop, since Stradivari's influence is unmistakable in his splendid instruments, also noted for the extraordinary beauty and transparency of their varnish.

The violin shown here belonged to the concert violinist, composer and well-known teacher Martin Marsick, who was born in Liège in 1848 and died in Paris in 1924. Marsick was a professor at the Paris Conservatoire, where, as Remy Principe states in his book on the violin, his pupils included Thibaud and Flesch. The instrument had previously been in the possession of a German collector from the Rhine valley. Joachim, a friend of this collector, was often his guest and would contentedly play the Montagnana at his summer residence on the banks of the river. Later, Leonid Kogan too had occasion to admire its tonal qualities.

The violin ultimately went to the firm of Max Möller in Amsterdam, whence it came to Italy. The belly is of best pine of medium grain. The back is made of two pieces of curly maple which has a very beautiful appearance and strikingly shows off the splendour of the varnish. In his assessment S. F. Sacconi describes the instrument as follows: 'This violin is the finest specimen I know of this master's work.' It is large in its format, though of moderate length, and has long Cs with pointed corners. The body, embellished with very delicate purfling, has ribs of moderate height. The varnish is of a warm golden orange, and unusually transparent; this is undoubtedly the best and most beautiful of the colours used by the Venetian violin-makers.

VIII. CARLO BERGONZI 'MISCHA PIASTRO'

Cremona, 1739 (ex Wurlitzer)

The violin shown here is a perfect example of this master's work. Bergonzi worked intuitively above all. In respect of the tonal quality and the timbre of his instruments he can be ranked between Stradivari and Guarneri del Gesù.

In 1939 this violin, at the time in the possession of Hill of London, was acquired by the firm of Rembert Wurlitzer in New York. It was then bought by the violinist and patron John T. Pratt and loaned to Mischa Piastro, a Russian soloist, who was well known as a pedagogue and as the teacher of Ricci, Persinger and Kulenkampff.

Piastro was also leader of the San Francisco Philharmonic Orchestra, and it was there that Toscanini heard him, and asked him to join his Philharmonic Orchestra in New York. John T. Pratt, moved by this honour, presented his Bergonzi to his friend Piastro. During Toscanini's American period, in any discussion of the finest sounds produced by violins and violinists, the first names to be mentioned would be those of the two Mischas: Elman and Piastro. After the latter's death, the instrument was once more acquired by the firm of Wurlitzer. It was kept for a long time in their private collection.

We have to thank that great but alas, short-lived connoisseur of violins, Simone Fernando Sacconi, for this violin's return to Italy. In his assessment for the firm of Wurlitzer, he wrote: 'The varnish is of a splendour that puts us in mind of the Berthier Strad, 1716, particularly as regards the belly; the tone is superb—no other Bergonzi that we know of possesses this sensational sound; it is an absolutely perfect concert instrument.'

The extremely fine scroll is generally acknowledged to be the work of Guarneri filius Andrea, who was the teacher of Bergonzi as well as of Guarneri del Gesù. Occasionally, though not often, makers of the time used to exchange certain parts, such as scrolls, amongst themselves when a violin had to be finished quickly.

The back is a single piece of maple with a small curl descending to the right. The pine of the belly is of medium grain, and is likewise very attractive. The ribs have a broad and slightly less pronounced curl, whilst the maple of the scroll has a smaller, fainter curl. The varnish, still present in abundance, is magnificent, luminous and of an intense orange-red colour.

Violin-makers consider this violin to be one of Bergonzi's finest and best preserved instruments. Unfortunately this master's work is very rarely found today: he was indisputably the greatest and most gifted of Antonio Stradivari's colleagues and of the pupils of Giuseppe Guarneri filius Andrea.

IX. SANCTUS SERAPHIN 'LACHMANN'

Venice, 1740 (ex Wurlitzer/Sacconi)

The original label of this violin bears the following note: 'Ad exemplar Antonii & Hieronimy Amati Cremonensium', and carries the brand mark of the Venetian maker on its back, near the end button. Despite the note on the label, the violin is a very personal example of the art of this celebrated maker, who was a native of Friuli. Sanctus Seraphin worked in Venice from 1717 to 1744. As soon as he felt that his powers were declining, he left the city. It is not known where he then settled, or where, in 1748, he died.

This violin dates from the maker's maturity and displays the unusually marked pointedness of the C corners that is characteristic of his work.

Very little is known of the instrument's early history, as is generally the case when an owner is forced into selling a masterpiece. The first American owner was possibly a Los Angeles violinist. In 1957 the instrument came into the hands of Erich Lachmann, a violin-maker of that city. Later it was evidently acquired by a collector in Seattle, Washington, being subsequently bought by the firm of Wurlitzer in New York, and the violin remained in their collection until its return to Italy. This violin was renowned in the United States for the warmth and carrying power of its tone, and for its splendid back which is made from slab-cut maple, so that the knots ('bird's eye' knots—'ad occhio di uccello') on this marvellously grained wood are particularly conspicuous.

The body has pronounced arching, and the fine purfling is particularly elegant. The splendid varnish is of an intense bright orange, such as was chosen by some Venetian makers as an alternative to red. Every detail of this violin speaks of craftsmanship of the highest quality. It possesses a wonderfully balanced tone and a distinguished timbre, so that it is capable of more than dominating a large orchestra; it is particularly well suited to gramophone recordings, because its tonal properties make it astonishingly 'micro-phonogenic'—a rare quality. The instrument is in a perfect state of preservation.

X. PETRUS GUARNERIUS II 'BARON KNOOP'
Venice, 1743 (ex Hammerle/Hottinger)

'The admirable combination of its wood and its varnish makes this extraordinary instrument the masterpiece of this supremely gifted artist.'

(Hottinger, Coll. Wurlitzer Inc., 1967)

Petrus Guarnerius was born in Cremona in 1695, and was the son of Giuseppe ('filius Joseph'). He was a pupil first of his father, then of his uncle Pietro in Mantua, before settling in Venice in 1725; here the enchanting beauty of his instruments—often inspired by the wild tumult of his emotions—exerted a strong influence on his contemporaries. The tone of this masterpiece of 1743 is truly sensational.

Baron Knoop of London was the first well-known owner of this prized instrument, at the end of the last century. After his death it found a worthy place in the collection of Theodor Hammerle, the great connoisseur from Vienna whose collection was famous throughout the world. When Hammerle too died, the violin was brought by his widow to Cremona where many famous violin-makers were celebrating the bicentenary of Stradivari's death. The instrument was entrusted to Simone Fernando Sacconi, who was at that time working for the New York firm of Emil Herman; it was thereupon acquired by the industrialist Henry Hottinger, already the possessor of the largest and most famous collection of classic Italian violins in America. In the catalogue of his collection there are some very beautiful colour reproductions of this Petrus Guarnerius. The Hottinger Collection was sold to the firm of Wurlitzer in 1967, and they dispersed it piece by piece. The '1743 Petrus Guarnerius' was kept, because it was acknowledged to be 'by far the master's most beautiful and perfect instrument'.

A Viennese description of the instrument from the end of the nineteenth century reads as follows: 'The Venetian Petrus Guarnerius (1743) from Baron Knoop's collection, and now in Hammerle's, is acknowledged to be that renowned maker's finest and most beautiful instrument. This violin is large in format, and has retained its splendid dark red Venetian varnish in abundance. The instrument has a tonal intensity and a timbre comparable to those of a Stradivari from his best period.' This violin is also mentioned in *The Guarneri Family* published by W. E. Hill & Sons.

XI. CARLO FERDINANDO LANDOLFI
'SIMONETTI'
Milan, 1751 (ex Hill/Werro)

Landolfi was an extremely fine and individual maker who was active during the great age of violin-making. He was born in 1714 in Milan and died in his native city in 1787 (or 1778?). His output includes both good and less fine instruments (his son and assistants probably collaborated with him), but all his instruments give proof of a certain personal touch, even though many of them call to mind the models of Guarneri del Gesù, and many of his cellos those of Pietro Guarneri of Mantua.

After an apprenticeship in Cremona, Landolfi moved to Milan in 1734. He occupied a workshop in the 'Contrada Santa Margherita, al Segno della Sirena', as the label of this violin tells us. Thus his situation in the metropolis of Lombardy was right at the centre of the city's hectic mercantile and artistic activities.

He chose his woods with care and often used superb varnishes of a sumptuous red hue which, now partly faded, is particularly striking on some of his instruments. According to Reade, Landolfi may be accounted the last of the classical master violin-makers to use Cremonese methods of construction and of compounding varnishes (see von Lütgendorff). His instruments were particularly appreciated in England.

The devotion Landolfi lavished on his best violins is remarkable. All of them express their maker's distinctive personality. Despite certain similarities to Guarneri del Gesù, Landolfi, who was considered a master of the art in Milan, went his own way, constantly improving with experience. In course of time he increased the arching of the belly in relation to the back; he took no particular trouble with the sound-holes, but carved the scroll in a graceful manner whilst at the same time making it smaller and broader than the usual shape. His instruments usually possess a full tone of great carrying power. On this account they are always valued by performers as excellent concert instruments. Flesch possessed a very fine Landolfi.

The early history of the violin depicted here is not known in detail. Recently it passed from Hill of London, where it was registered as Number W 922, to Werro in Berne. A few years ago, it finally returned from that city to its native Italy.

The instrument was made in Milan in 1751 and is in an extremely good state of preservation. The beautiful belly is in two parts and has pronounced open grain. The plain maple back, too, is in two parts; the ribs and scroll have a faint curl. The edges are distinctly thrown into relief and lend plasticity to the instrument's appearance, this being particularly emphasised by the purfling. The well-preserved and abundant varnish is of a strong dark red colour, calling to mind many a brilliant varnish of the Venetian school.

XII. FERDINANDO GAGLIANO FIL. NIC.
'GIOCONDA DE VITO'

Naples, 1762 (ex Kalman Ronay)

This excellent concert instrument was made by Ferdinando, eldest son of Nicolo Gagliano, who was probably born in Naples in 1724, dying in that city in 1781.

Ferdinando's instruments are broader and more massive than those of his father, and are also worked in a far more individual way, as with this 1762 violin.

The maple back, made from a single piece, is marked by a small curl, this being more pronounced in the ribs and plainer in the superb scroll. The belly is of pine of medium grain. The varnish is a warm golden brown. The instrument is 35.5 centimetres long and has been preserved completely intact.

This violin was owned by the Russian virtuoso Kalman Ronay, who brought his uncle Leopold Auer's violin school from St Petersburg to London at the end of the nineteenth century. Ronay played the instrument at all his concerts, and left it to his pupil Albert Sandler, who at the beginning of the century became the most famous English virtuoso of his time. The latter parted with it only when he managed to acquire a Bergonzi. Various owners followed, before the violin reached Hill of London.

Gioconda de Vito acquired the instrument in 1956, and was enthusiastic about its tone, which she described as 'warm, balanced and penetrating'; she played this instrument during the final years of her brilliant career, after she had given back the 'Tuscan' Stradivari to the Accademia Nazionale di Santa Cecilia in Rome which had lent it to her.

XIII. JOH. BAPT. GUADAGNINI 'JOACHIM'

Parma, 1767 (ex Sennhauser)

G. B. Guadagnini's are now among the most sought-after instruments on account of their overall quality and because they are among the last products of the great Cremonese violin-makers. According to Sacconi, this violin is typical of Guadagnini's Parma period. At that time he still made mention on his labels of the fact that his origins were with the Cremonese school. (Fridolin Hamma believes it possible that this violin may date from the master's Milan period.)

The first known owner of this instrument was Joseph Joachim. He played it between 1854 and 1866 in Hanover as leader of the Royal Orchestra, as well as later during his first years as a violin teacher at the Berlin Academy of Music. Although in Berlin he enjoyed the use of a Stradivari which he acquired, and subsequently of another which was presented to him, he never ceased to recommend Guadagnini's instruments to pupils who were unable to afford expensive violins. (See Fritz Meyer, who mentions this violin.) The present-day demand for good Guadagninis confirms Joachim's almost prophetic recommendation. (See also *The Strad* No. 867, 1962.)

Doring mentions this instrument as being Joachim's 'one-time solo violin during the entire period of his activity at Hanover'. It is illustrated in F. Hamma. From Joachim this violin passed to Hamma of Stuttgart, then to the Swiss collector Sennhauser in St Gallen, and later to a performer and teacher at the Zurich Conservatoire, Professor Marti. After her death the famous violin returned to Italy via the Zurich firm of Hug. Every soloist who has played on this concert instrument has been enchanted by its fresh and full tone and by the ease with which it responds on all its strings.

The fine varnish is a pleasing orange-brown in colour. The violin is of large size and of average length. The back, in two parts and marked by a small curl, is of particular interest since it is made of Italian maple. The instrument is in a perfect state of preservation.

XIV. JOH. BAPT. GUADAGNINI 'KLEYNENBERG'
Turin, 1783 (ex Molina/Ben Senescu)

This violin is a splendid example of the master's work during his Turin period. It is now back from the United States, where it was described by connoisseurs as the finest of all the known Guadagninis in America.

It is not known how and when the instrument went to America. Peter Kleynenberg, whose name it bears, bought it from Carl Becker of Chicago in 1924. It was then acquired by the Chicago firm of Lewis and Son, and from there passed into the possession of Carlos Molina and later of Ben Senescu, two well-known soloists of the time. It was S. F. Sacconi, with his infinite devotion to the art of violin-making, and the firm of Wurlitzer who made it possible for this superb instrument to return to its native land.

Doring mentions that the violin has a powerful tone. It is a masterpiece, and proves that at 72 the maker was still in full possession of his creative faculties. Guadagnini was able to live in freedom from hardship—he found a patron in the person of Count Cozio di Salabue, a passionate lover of the art of violin-making. Thus, like the masters of Cremona and Venice, Guadagnini was able to buy valuable woods and costly ingredients for his varnishes.

This violin is in excellent condition; it still bears its original label. The splendid transparent varnish, much of which has survived and is well preserved, is a warm dark red. The back, of quarter-cut maple, is marked by an irregular medium curl. The belly, likewise in two halves, is of fine grain at the centre opening towards the flanks. The ribs and the scroll are also of maple. The lower part of the sound-holes has the peardrop shape characteristic of Guadagnini.

The tone of this instrument is warm and has great carrying power, as with the best of Stradivari's violins. Hill's certificate states: 'The violin is an exceptionally fine and typical example of G. B. Guadagnini's final, Turin period.'

Bibliography to the Plates

De Piccolellis, *Liutai antichi e moderni*, Florence, 1885.

E. N. Doring, *The Guadagnini Family*, Chicago, 1949.

H. K. Goodkind, *Violin Iconography of A. Stradivari*, Larchmont, New York, 1972.

F. Hamma, *Meisterwerke italienischer Geigenbaukunst*, Stuttgart, 1931.

W. Hamma, *Meister italienischer Geigenbaukunst*, Stuttgart, 1964.

G. Hart, *Le Violon, ses luthiers célèbres et leurs imitateurs*, Paris.

W. Henley, *Antonio Stradivari: His Life and Instruments*, Brighton, 1961.

A. E., A. F. and W. H. Hill, *The Guarneri Family*, London, 1931; new ed., 1965.

von Lütgendorff, *Die Geigen und Lautenmacher*, 1913.

F. Meyer, *Berühmte Geigen und ihre Schicksale*, Cologne, 1919.

R. Principe, *Il Violino*, Milan, 1951.

S. F. Sacconi, *I 'Segreti' di Stradivari*, Cremona, 1972.

A. Vidal, *La Lutherie et les luthiers*, Paris, 1889.